Renaissance Spain
in Its Literary Relations
with England and France

Renaissance Spain in Its Literary Relations with England and France

A Critical Bibliography

Compiled by

Hilda U. Stubbings

VANDERBILT *University Press*
Nashville

Copyright © 1968, 1969 by Hilda Urén Stubbings.
Standard Book Number 8265–1142–2
Library of Congress Catalogue Card Number 70–89143
Printed in the United States of America by
Heritage Printers, Inc., Charlotte, North Carolina
Bound by Nicholstone Book Bindery
Nashville, Tennessee

To Gerald E. Wade

Preface

It is surprising that no bibliography, even an incomplete one, exists for Spanish-French, Spanish-English literary relations. Scholars and students of Hispanic literature as well as those in comparative literature have noted this gap at various times; this bibliography is an effort partly to fill the gap. In making this statement, of course, I do not overlook the useful bibliographies in literary relations such as Lois Strong Gaudin's *Bibliography of Franco-Spanish Literary Relations*, which was a pioneer in the field. Miss Gaudin's work, however, does not include English literature and is of a more general nature than the present compilation. Too, it appeared in 1930 and has not been revised; therefore, it does not reflect the great amount of scholarship which has been done since that time.

This work, of course, does not pretend to be definitive. I am acutely aware that my efforts to compile a bibliography that aims even at partial completeness for this large an area must remain imperfect, and I beg the researcher's indulgence for the lacunae which he is certain to find. Future bibliographers will, I hope, offer added materials, especially since the field of comparative literature is continually expanding.

Although I hope that this bibliography will be of assistance to scholars in the fields of Anglo-Romance literary relations everywhere, it has been compiled with especial attention to the needs of students of comparative literature in the United States. The bibliographical items include only books, monographs, and articles which can be found in at least the larger American libraries. I realize that this will eliminate reference to much valuable scholarly research available in foreign libraries only, but perhaps the accessibility of the materials included here will compensate the American student for that disadvantage. Perhaps, too, this explanation will relieve the present compiler from the charge of negligence. It has been my frequent experience to find that a bibliographical reference which promised usefulness because of its relevant title has proved to be of little practical value because the source material was difficult to find. Too, I have had the experience of following up a bibliographical reference found in a so-called "comparative" bibliography, only to find that the book or article was not truly comparative at all and that I had gone to much trouble to find something I could not use. One of the criteria for the inclusion of any item in this work has been that it should represent some significant relationship between two of the literatures, Spanish and French or Spanish and English, or a comparison among the three. Thus, I hope that the present bibliography can have real usefulness for the researcher.

My plan for the compilation has been based upon the following considerations:

1) Each item deals with some phase of Renaissance Spanish influence, in literature or culture, on the literature and/or culture of England and France during the sixteenth, seventeenth, and eighteenth centuries. "Culture" here is taken in its broad sense and is not restricted to art but refers to the civilization in general. "Renaissance" is taken to refer to the period which corresponds roughly to that time which is known among Spanish scholars as the "Golden Age" of Spanish literature and culture. Since there is some disagreement among scholars concerning the limits of this period, I should no doubt explain how I have interpreted it for the purposes of this bibliography. The problem of identifying this period conclusively has been well summed up by Friederich and Malone as follows:

The duration of the Spanish Golden Century differs according to the viewpoints of various critics; it might be said to have lasted during the reign of Philip II, Philip III, and Philip IV (1556–1665); or again it may be said to have begun with the birth of Cervantes (1547) and to have ended with the death of Lope de Vega (1635). Calderón lived somewhat beyond the peak of the Golden Age, just as Tasso lived beyond the apex of the Italian Renaissance. Scholars with an eye for well-fitting dates might enjoy the neat succession of literary hegemonies arrived at if the end of the Golden Age of Spain is indicated at the time of Lope's death in 1635 and the beginning of the Classical Period of France is said to have started with Corneille's Cid in 1636.[1]

I have not worked with "an eye for well-fitting dates," but have chosen to widen the limits to include material which considers the impact of works or events which came before the earliest date mentioned above (1547) if they created an effect that was strongly felt in England

[1] Werner P. Friederich and David Henry Malone, *Outline of Comparative Literature* (Chapel Hill: University of North Carolina Press, 1954), p. 107.

or France up until what is known as the height of the neo-classical age. At the other end of the spectrum, I shall accept the date of Calderón's death (1789) as the virtual end of the Golden Age in Spain, since there is much evidence of Calderón's influence in the other two countries.

One cogent reason for pushing back the early limits of the period to be covered in this bibliography is that the effect of such works as *La Celestina* (1499) and *Amadís de Gaula* (1508), among others, became apparent in England and France only after they had been made available to readers by translators, or after some historical event (such as the marriage of Louis XIII to the daughter of Felipe III) occurred to focus attention on Spain. Too, many Spanish works lay neglected in foreign countries until later writers discovered inspiration in them. I have tried to gather together the works of Spanish literature which have been most influential during the three centuries I have chosen to treat, and in this manner I have sought to direct the attention of the student to the importance of the Spanish contribution during these years.

2) The items may be written by authors of any nation as long as they approach the subject from the viewpoint of the Spanish contribution and write in Spanish, English, or French. The material is, however, derived primarily from works published in Spain, France, England, and the United States.

3) General works which include significant amounts of material on the subject are included, often with a note to the reader to consult the indices of the works, if the comparative material is not sufficiently concentrated to make citing page numbers practicable.

4) Occasionally references which provide valuable insights for the understanding of the social backgrounds are included if these help in the interpretation of the literature. An understanding of the Inquisition, for example, fits into this category, since it spread into the three countries concerned, with its greatest impact occurring in Spain. These works are not necessarily comparative.

5) Material which deals exclusively with listings of translations of Spanish works has not been included, since it is accessible elsewhere. Only if a certain translation is particularly important in its influence on the creation of subsequent original works or if a translation has become a subject for extended discussion among scholars has it been considered useful here.

6) References to Spanish-American or Portuguese literature are not included: the items are confined to the geographical area of peninsular Spain.

7) No effort has been made to cover thoroughly an area which has already been exhaustively treated, although certain items which seem to be of especial comparative interest have been included. Such an area is the Don Juan theme; for this subject the reader is directed to Armand E. Singer's compilation, *The Don Juan Theme, Versions and Criticisms: A Bibliography* (Morgantown: West Virginia University Press, 1965).

This bibliography is divided into two general classifications: Books and Monographs and Journal Articles. The first category includes dissertations, addresses, and essays taken from collections.

Entries are numbered consecutively for ease of location within the work; therefore, multiple references to certain authors, works, or subjects found in the index will be quickly accessible. Cross references have often been made within the entries if certain works complement each other in ways which make knowledge of them advantageous to the researcher.

An extensive index is provided for maximum usefulness to the student and for his easy reference. In it will be found references to the authors and titles of works listed; titles, persons, and authors mentioned within the commentaries; as well as references to such concepts as "Gongorism," "leyenda negra," and so forth. In addition, certain genres and themes are listed so that a researcher pursuing a general subject may be assisted in finding pertinent material. Certain bibliographies on special subjects are listed under the heading "Bibliographies."

The commentaries are designed to assist the student in determining whether or not a particular book or article will meet the requirements of his research project. The length of the commentary is not necessarily an indication of this compiler's judgment of the publication's merits, for in the case of a whole volume devoted to a certain subject—Spanish-French relations, for example—a summary would do little justice to the contents or would grow to unwieldy proportions. In the case of a monograph or article, where the area of focus is less broad, I have sought to give the reader an indication of the salient points brought out by the author so that he may be stimulated to explore a new area or to continue investigations to which a summary may allude. In this way it is hoped that the present bibliography may prove to be a stimulus to future scholarship.

It is a pleasure to express my appreciation to those who have assisted me in the completion of this work. Many thanks are due to all who have patiently read the manuscript in the various stages of its preparation. Needless to say, any errors that it may contain are solely my own. I wish to thank Dr. Donald McGrady of the University of California at Santa Barbara, Miss Eleanor Anne Hurst of the duPont-Ball Library at Stetson University, Mr. Jesse Ray Jones of the Research Library at the University of Florida, and others for their valuable suggestions, as well as Dr. John M. Aden, Dr. Ruth Grace, and Dr. Phillip H. Rhein, all of Vanderbilt University, for their interest and encouragement.

I am grateful to my family and to friends (with especial thanks to Mrs. William M. Colbert Jr. and Mr. and Mrs. Gregory Makris) who have added their labors to mine along the way, for their assistance in the organization of the project and for their continuing interest. To Shawn and to my husband, George, who were always there to help, I offer my hope that they may feel rewarded for their efforts.

Willamette University
Salem, Oregon   H. U. S.
June 1969

Abbreviations

BA	Books Abroad
BH	Bulletin Hispanique
BHS	Bulletin of Hispanic Studies
BPLQ	Boston Public Library Quarterly
BSS	Bulletin of Spanish Studies
CL	Comparative Literature
CW	Catholic World
DA	Dissertation Abstracts
DS	Dix-Septième Siècle
EAP	English Association Pamphlet
ELN	English Language Notes
FoR	Fortnightly Review
FR	French Review
HAHR	Hispanic American Historical Review
HLQ	Huntington Library Quarterly
HR	Hispanic Review
JDS	Journal des Savants
JEGP	Journal of English and Germanic Philology
LLR	Les Lettres Romanes
LTLS	London Times Literary Supplement
ML	Modern Languages
MLJ	Modern Language Journal
MLN	Modern Language Notes
MLQ	Modern Language Quarterly
MLR	Modern Language Review
MP	Modern Philology
NQ	Notes and Queries
NRFH	Nueva Revista de Filología Hispánica
PBA	Proceedings of the British Academy

PMLA   Publications of the Modern Language Association of America
PQ   Philological Quarterly
RB   Revue Bleue
RDM   Revue des Deux Mondes
ReE   Revista de España
REH   Revista de Estudios Hispánicos
ReL   Revista de Literatura
RES   Review of English Studies
RF   Romanische Forschungen
RFE   Revista de Filología Española
RH   Revue Hispanique
RHLF   Revue d'Histoire Littéraire de la France
RJ   Romanistisches Jahrbuch
RLC   Revue de Littérature Comparée
RLR   Revue des Langues Romanes
RO   Revista de Occidente
RR   Romanic Review
SP   Studies in Philology
SQ   Shakespeare Quarterly
SS   Shakespeare Survey
WVUB   West Virginia University Bulletin

Contents

Renaissance Spain
in Its Literary Relations
with England and France

Books and Monographs

[1]   Alexander, Jean. "Parallel Tendencies in English and Spanish Tragedy in the Renaissance," in *Studies in Comparative Literature*, Waldo F. NcNeir, editor. Baton Rouge: Louisiana State University Press, 1962.

      The author surveys the dramas of England and Spain and finds them similar in orientation, because of their appeal to the popular audience, and similar in their use of dramatic devices. Miss Alexander finds, however, that the English drama is not so simply unified as the Spanish, owing to the originality of mind of various English dramatists.

[2]   Alonso, Dámaso, y Carlos Bousoño. *Seis Calas en la expressión literaria española*. Madrid: Editorial Gredos, 1963.

      Six studies which systematically analyze the structure of certain literary works of the late Renaissance to discover correlations among them, with Gongorism as the focus of attention. Of especial interest is "Poesía correlativa inglesa en los siglos XVI y XVII," pp. 327–377.

[3]   Armas y Cárdenas, José de. *Cervantes en la literatura inglesa; conferencia leída en el Ateneo de Madrid el día 8 de mayo de 1916*. Madrid: Imprenta Renacimiento, 1916.

      The author contends that "es innegable que [Cervantes] adquirió un conocimiento muy preciso de aquel país [Inglaterra] y una gran estimación para sus méritos." Edwin B. Knowles, in his essay "Cervantes and English Literature" (see entry 75) considers this to be rather unsound, since much of it is based on conjecture.

[4]   ————. *Ensayos críticos de literatura inglesa y española*. Madrid: V. Suárez, 1910.

"Calderón en Inglaterra," pp. 151–158: a short review of Calderón's popularity in England, much less great than that of Cervantes, Armas notes, but of considerable proportions, as shown by the frequent translations of Calderón's plays, beginning in 1667 with George Digby's translation of *No siempre lo peor es cierto*.

"Moreto," pp. 185–195: Armas believes that Moreto may be classed with Shakespeare, Cervantes, and Molière as authors who portray most vividly the customs and emotions of the times in which they lived and who are the most penetrating in their descriptions of "el género humano." He finds that Moreto is the Spanish dramatist who most closely resembles Molière.

"Antoine de Brunel y su viaje a España en 1665," pp. 235–281. Noting with disapproval the greater attention accorded travel accounts written later than Brunel's, Armas sees Brunel as a more objective and perspicacious observer of Spanish life in the seventeenth century, for such commentators as Mme d'Aulnoy and the Marquis de Villars, he believes, were deceived by appearances or carried away by their own imaginations. In setting forth Brunel's analysis of the causes of Spain's decadence during this era, Armas provides the reader with useful insights into the understanding of the Spanish literature of this era and later ones. Of interest in relation to English history is the author's explanation of Cromwell's role in Spain's fall.

These essays are interestingly written and show both originality and a wide knowledge of the subjects.

[5] Arnold, Morris Le Roy, *The Soliloquies of Shakespeare: a Study in Technic*. ("Columbia University Studies in English.") New York: Columbia University Press, 1911.

Arnold considers the use of the soliloquy by Shakespeare and his contemporaries in Spain and France and includes material on the development of the soliloquy as a dramatic technique as it is found in the works of Lope de Vega and others. To find passages on Spanish drama, consult the index under the name of the author or play being studied.

[6] Astrana Marín, Luis. *Cervantinas y otros ensayos*. Madrid: Afrodisio Aguado, S.A., 1944.

"Shakespeare interpretado con Cervantes," pp. 353–356. An interesting sidelight on the way textual problems may be solved, this essay tells how one scholar, Henry Thomas, "decoded" a phrase ("Castiliano vulgo") in Shakespeare's *Twelfth Night* that had puzzled scholars for years. Through a clue in Cervantes' *El Licenciado vidriera* Thomas was able to resolve the problem.

[7] ———. *El Cortejo de Minerva*. Madrid: Espasa-Calpe, S.A., 1930.
Citing Cervantes as the greatest creator of values, Astrana finds in the works of writers of other countries besides Spain a lively appreciation of Cervantes' genius. These writers include John Fletcher (pp. 120–127), and Alain Lesage (pp. 135–142). Of interest also are remarks on Quevedo, Shakespeare, and Voltaire, pp. 143–172.

[8] Aubrun, Charles Vincent. *La Comédie espagnole (1600–1680)*. ("Publications de la faculté des lettres et sciences humaines de Paris, Sorbonne. Série 'Études et Méthodes,' " tome 14.) Paris: Presses Universitaires de France, 1966.
A readable and scholarly analysis of the *comedia* which does not treat of influences in depth but does mention them as the various authors are discussed. The indices contain names of authors and titles of works, but no subject headings; bibliography is found in the *Préface* and within the footnotes.

[9] Bardon, Maurice. *Don Quichotte en France au XVIIᵉ et au XVIIIᵉ siècle, 1605–1815*. 2 vols. Illustrated. Paris: H. Champion, 1931.
A thorough study of the fortunes of Cervantes' masterpiece in France in all its aspects. It contains copious footnotes and a useful bibliography which includes texts of *Don Quijote*, a list of translations into French, adaptations and imitations, historical and critical studies, and pertinent dictionaries, encyclopedias, and manuals. "A definitive work," says Esther J. Crooks in her essay "Translations of Cervantes into French," included in *Cervantes Across the Centuries*, edited by Flores and Benardete. (See entry 43.)

[10] Baret, Eugène. *Les Troubadours et leur influence sur la littérature du midi de l'Europe, avec des extraits et des pièces rares ou inédites.* 2d ed. Paris: Didier et Cie, 1867.

Chapter VII, "De l'imitation espagnole en France au XVIIe siècle," pp. 285–334. Baret sees Spanish letters as exerting a strong influence in France through the works of Castro, Quevedo, Pérez, Alarcón, Tirso de Molina, Lope de Vega, Padre Francisco de Isla, and others. He is thought to be the first to note Corneille's debt to Spanish literature. An appendix gives several examples of French translations from Spanish authors and the original texts.

[11] Bataillon, Marcel. *"La Célestine" selon Fernando de Rojas.* Paris: Librairie Marcel Didier, 1961.

An excellent study of *La Celestina* which has the thesis that this novel formed the prototype of a "genre de moralité," and that by studying its imitations we may understand the prototype. Chapter VIII, pp. 226–250, views the play in its historical perspective. The author includes notes but no subject index, although there is an index to passages cited from *La Celestina*.

[12] ———. *Le Roman picaresque.* Paris: La Renaissance du Livre, 1931.

The author remarks that although the *roman picaresque* is not exclusively Spanish, its birthplace was Spain; he goes on to analyze three principal Spanish picaresque works: *Lazarillo de Tormes, Guzmán de Alfarache,* and *El Buscón.* The introduction to the book (pp. 1–39) affords a useful survey of the European development of the picaresque novel. The work contains footnotes but no index.

[13] Bell, Aubrey F. G. *Cervantes.* Norman: University of Oklahoma Press, 1947.

This book has no section which concentrates on comparative aspects, but Bell makes use of his extensive knowledge to tie in Spanish literary figures with those of other nations. Fortunately, his index of names amply provides the student with the page numbers of specific references, even short ones. Provided is a bibliography of works on Cervantes, including some comparative studies.

[14] Bomli, P. W. *La Femme dans l'Espagne du siècle d'or.* The Hague: Martinus Nijhoff, 1950.

The author uses contemporary literature and travel accounts to study the position of women in Golden Age Spain and to note the characteristics of their lives in different social strata. Bomli admits that his sources are scanty, a principal one being the *Voyage* of Mme d'Aulnoy (of which the authenticity has been doubted). This study concerns itself mainly with young women and those in the upper classes. It overemphasizes the decadence of Spain. A good index makes the book easy to use. Reviewed by A. A. Parker in *BHS*, XXVIII (1951). (See entry 210 for comments on the authenticity of Mme d'Aulnoy's travel account.)

[15] Boughner, Daniel C. *The Braggart in Renaissance Comedy: A Study in Comparative Drama from Aristophanes to Shakespeare.* Minneapolis: University of Minnesota Press, 1954.

A thematic study which covers the comedy of Renaissance Spain, England, France, and Italy, as well as the classical backgrounds which were important in the development of this form. Material on French drama in the seventeenth century is included. Joseph E. Gillet writes in *HR*, XXIV (1956), that "the Spanish part is competently done" and that it is "interesting . . . well-organized . . . and scholarly."

[16] Bray, René. *La Préciosité et les précieux.* Paris: Editions Albin Michel, 1948.

Chapter VI, "Répères étrangères de Lily à Góngora," pp. 85–98. An interesting analysis of the parallels to be found in *préciosité* in France, marinism in Italy, *conceptismo* in Spain, and euphuism in England. The author sees the Spanish and English varieties of this phenomenon developing outside the works of Góngora and Lyly, but he also sees all these manifestations linked together by a common taste for the baroque within the four nations.

[17] Brody, Ervin Constantin. "Events of the Russian Time of Troubles in Two Baroque Dramas: Lope de Vega's *El gran duque de Moscovia* and John Fletcher's *The Loyal Subject.*"

Unpublished Ph.D. dissertation, Columbia University, 1967.

Lope and Fletcher use the same "Demetrius legend," which grew out of a turbulent period in Russian history (1598–1613) under Ivan the Terrible. Brody examines the two plays to observe the use of the theme by each poet and sees Lope as treating it in a "typically Spanish" way, making it a eulogy of family life, while Fletcher's play presents no such unifying concept. Brody sees Lope's plays *El gran duque de Moscovia* and *El duque de Viseo* as literary sources for *The Loyal Subject*, along with English historical works. The study concludes by delineating the baroque elements in each play. (Abstract appears in *DA*, XXVIII-A [1967], 1388-A.)

[18] Brunetière, Ferdinand. *Études critiques sur l'histoire de la littérature française.* Paris: Librairie Hachette et Cie, 1904.

"Le Sage," pp. 63–120. Although Brunetière gives credit to Spain for some of Lesage's inspiration in *Gil Blas*, he prefers to believe that the Spanish picaresque novel owes more of its fame to the French writer, just as the story of the Cid owes more to Corneille than to Castro. Brunetière comments, "Voilà tantôt deux cent cinquante ans que l'Europe ne connait à peu près du dramaturge espagnol que ce qu'il a convenu au poète français d'en imiter, pour le perfectionner." He does admit that the French writers imitated the Spanish.

"L'influence de l'Espagne dans la littérature française," pp. 51–71. Brunetière sees the role of Spain greater than that of any other country in its effect upon French literature. This statement is criticized by Farinelli in his *Divagaciones hispánicas* (II, 15-16), for he is convinced that the Italian influence is greater. (See entry 40.)

[19] Carayon, Marcel. "Les trois poèmes de Crashaw sur Sainte-Thérèse," in *Hommage à Ernest Martinenche, études hispaniques et américaines.* Paris: Editions d'Artrey, 1939.

Carayon sees the influence of Saint Teresa as crucial in the development of Richard Crashaw's thought as it is revealed in his poetry; here he presents his translations into French of Crashaw's three "hymns" to the Spanish mystic.

[20]   Carrasco Urgoiti, María Soledad. *El Moro de Granada en la literatura (del siglo XV al XX)*. Madrid: Revista de Occidente, 1956.

Miss Carrasco studies the impact of the Spanish "galanterie" on seventeenth-century literature and society, concentrating chiefly on Mlle de Scudéry's *Almahide*, in which the Moorish theme was used. Some attention is given, too, to Voiture, Mme de La Fayette, Mme de Villedieu, and Quinault in regard to this theme.

[21]   Castro, Américo. "El Don Juan de Tirso y el de Molière como personajes barrocos," in *Hommage à Ernest Martinenche, études hispaniques et américaines*. Paris: Editions d'Artrey, 1939.

An analysis of the "barroco" style and its development as a Spanish literary characteristic, with a comparison between Tirso's style and that of Molière, showing the changes in French style that are attributable to the Spanish influence.

[22]   Chancerel, Léon. *Panorama du théâtre des origines à nos jours*. Paris: Librairie Armand Colin, 1955.

The author proposes to give a panoramic view of the history of French drama and in so doing includes a look at Spanish influences under the headings "Les autos sacramentales" (pp. 40–45), and "Au pays du 'gracioso'" (pp. 141–144). There is neither index nor bibliography, but the textual notes contain references to other works on the drama. Useful as a guide to further research.

[23]   Chandler, Frank Wadleigh. *Romances of Roguery: An Episode in the History of the Novel*. ("Columbia University Studies in Literature.") 2 vols. New York: The Macmillan Company, 1899.

Chandler finds the original of the picaresque novel in the rogue story of *Lazarillo de Tormes*. He shows how this genre moves into other European countries after its inception in Spain, analyzes the social outlook of the *pícaro*, and examines the structure and elements of the picaresque as a literary phenomenon through its flowering and decadence. The author provides a useful bibliography which enhances the value of this study.

[24] ————. *The Literature of Roguery*. 2 vols. Boston and New York: Houghton, Mifflin and Company, 1907.

Chandler defines the type of literature that he labels "the anatomy of roguery and criminal biography" and finds its source in mid-sixteenth-century Spain as *Lazarillo de Tormes* appeared. Its spirit, he finds, derives in part from social conditions, in part from a recoil from chivalric literature. This study takes as points of departure both the literary and sociological backgrounds of the picaresque in the various European countries, especially England and France. Each chapter is enhanced in value by the addition of a bibliography, and the entire work is indexed according to authors and titles at the end of Vol. II.

[25] Chaplyn, Marjorie A. *Le Roman mauresque en France de "Zayde" au dernier "Abencérage."* Paris: A. Nizet et M. Bastard, 1928.

This work is organized around the theme of the popularity of books based upon the subject of the Moor in Spain: Part I —"Le Roman mauresque en France au XVIIe siècle"; Part II—"Le Roman mauresque en France au XVIIIe siècle." In Part I attention is focused on the works of Mlle de Scudéry, Mme de La Fayette, and Mme de Villedieu. The carefulness of the analyses makes this study valuable for the knowledge of an area which demonstrates the close intellectual ties of Spain and France.

[26] Chasles, Philarète. *Études sur l'Espagne et sur les influences de la littérature espagnole en France et en Italie*. Paris, 1860.

A pioneer work in the field of comparative literature by a master of French literary criticism, this study also includes Spanish influences on English literature, for which it will be necessary to consult the index under the writer being studied.

[27] Chaunu, Huguette, and Pierre Chaunu. "Le Climat des rapports Franco-Espagnols à Cadiz dans la seconde moitié du XVIIe siècle," in *Mélanges offerts à Marcel Bataillon, Bulletin Hispanique*, Tome LXIV bis. Bordeaux: Féret et Felc, 1962.

The decline of Spain's literary grandeur followed the decline of her political strength; the rise of France under Louis XIV and the subsequent French literary dictatorship are corollaries of this change in Spanish fortunes, as the authors of this article point out. Valuable for the understanding of the politico-literary relationships of the period 1650–1700.

[28]   Cioranescu, Alejandro. "Calderón y el teatro clásico francés," in *Estudios de literatura española y comparada*. Canary Islands: Universidad de la Laguna, 1954.

The author examines ten of Calderón's plays from the viewpoint of their influence on French drama; he sees Calderón as inspiring such French writers as D'Ouville, Boisrobert, Brosse, Scarron, Lambert, Thomas Corneille, and Quinault. It is the opinion of Arnold G. Reichenberger that these essays are "well-written" and "based on a firm theory of literature." (*CL*, VIII, 1956.)

[29]   Claretie, Léo. *Lesage romancier, d'après de nouveaux documents.* (*Le Roman en France au début du XVIIIᵉ siècle.*) Paris: Armand Colin et Cie, 1890.

Spanish influences on Lesage are treated on pp. 148–261. Admitting that one cannot speak of Lesage without speaking "un peu" of Spain, Claretie avers that he has endeavored to be impartial. He attributes Lesage's interest in all things Spanish to the prevailing fashion of the day when, since Spain had captured the political hegemony of Europe, all courtiers learned to speak Spanish. Claretie provides a thorough and readable account of Lesage's attitudes toward Spain, including also the attitudes of some Spanish critics toward Lesage.

[30]   Clarke, Butler. "The Spanish Rogue Story (Novelas de Pícaros)," in *Studies in European Literature*. The Taylorian Lectures, series one. Oxford: The Clarendon Press, 1930.

Calling the *pícaro* a universal type, the irresponsible product of a state of society and a primitive man in an artificial environment, Clarke notes the lasting appeal of the picaresque novel as he traces its rise and decline in Spain and touches upon its vogue in other lands.

[31] Coutu, Sister Albert Cécile. *Hispanism in France from Morel-Fatio to the Present (Circa 1875–1950).* ("The Catholic University of America Studies in Romance Languages and Literatures," Vol. XLIV.) Washington, D.C.: Catholic University of America Press, 1954.

A valuable source book for research into publications on Spanish subjects by French authors. The author rounds off her work with a bibliographical appendix containing titles of books by the *hispanisants* whose writings she considers in the body of the text. A selective bibliography also furnishes further information on these scholars. An index is provided.

[32] Crockett, Arnold Kelly. "The Picaresque Tradition in English Fiction to 1770." Unpublished Ph.D. dissertation, University of Illinois, 1954.

An investigation into English popular literature of the sixteenth, seventeenth, and eighteenth centuries as a major source of the picaresque for eighteenth-century English novelists, especially Fielding and Smollett. Crockett minimizes the importance of foreign models, pointing out several differences between English and foreign picaresque heroes and characterizing the picaresque novel in England not as a reaction against chivalric romances or a protest against social evils but as a work having a greater emphasis on morality. (Abstract appears in *DA*, XIV [1954], 355 f.)

[33] Crooks, Esther J. *The Influence of Cervantes in France in the Seventeenth Century.* ("Johns Hopkins Studies in Romance Literatures and Languages," extra volume IV.) Baltimore: Johns Hopkins University Press, 1931.

A thorough work which includes several sections treating the following subjects: references to Cervantes and his works in France; influences of Cervantes upon the poetry, novels, and plays of seventeenth-century France; influence of *Don Quijote* and *Las Novelas ejemplares* upon the French plays at this time; influence of Cervantes' drama upon the French drama. The last chapter contains Miss Crooks' general conclusions. The work includes textual notes, a lengthy bibliography, and an index.

[34]   ————. "Translations of Cervantes into French," in *Cervantes Across the Centuries*, edited by Angel Flores and M. J. Benardete. New York: The Dryden Press, 1947.

Miss Crooks considers *Don Quijote* in the light of French interpretations as well as translations and shows that up to the age of Louis XV, Cervantes' works were well received; with the waning of Spain's political power, however, the French became more critical of Spanish literature. In general, the French thought of *Don Quijote* as an amusing tale or a powerful literary satire.

[35]   Cross, Wilbur P. *The History of Henry Fielding*. 3 vols. New Haven: Yale University Press, 1918.

Vol. I, Chapter 12—"Joseph Andrews." Stating that Fielding took Cervantes for his model in writing *Joseph Andrews* (as Fielding notes on the title page), Cross finds examples of the correspondences between the characters of Don Quijote and Joseph Andrews but concludes, "Fielding was so saturated with Cervantes that analysis, beyond exteriors, is rendered almost helpless." He sees the character of Don Quijote reappear in the portrayal of another Fielding character, Parson Adams. This work has a bibliography of all of Fielding's writings; Vol. III contains an index to all volumes. Various other references to Spanish writings may be found by consulting Cross' index.

[36]   Daireaux, Max. *Collection Cervantes*. (Temps et Visages.) Paris: Desclée de Brouwer, 1948.

Chapter 16—"La Vie posthume de *Don Quichotte*." A rapid survey of the many ways in which *Don Quijote* has affected the literature of other European nations, especially in regard to the development of English humor. Daireaux praises Maurice Bardon's *Don Quichotte en France aux XVIIe et XVIIIe siècles*. (See entry 9.)

[37]   Demogeot, Jacques. *Histoire de la littérature française depuis ses origines jusqu'à nos jours*. Paris: Librairie Hachette et Cie, 1874.

Chapter XIX, pp. 353–357. "Influence de l'Espagne."

Demogeot notes the importance of the role played by Antonio Pérez in France after he was chosen by Henry IV to give him Spanish lessons. Chapter XXX, pp. 373–382, presents material on Hardy's use of Cervantes' and Lope de Vega's works as well as on Corneille's debt to Spain.

In general Demogeot believes that Spanish influence was deleterious rather than beneficial. His presentation of literary history is biased in favor of classicism as interpreted by Boileau, and under this influence he calls England, Spain, and Italy "trois ennemies" of French literature. This work has an index of subjects and proper names.

[38]   Dubech, Lucien, *et al. Histoire générale illustrée du théâtre.* 5 vols. Illustrated. Paris: Librairie de France, 1931–1934.

Vol. III, pp. 1–226, "Le Théâtre espagnol." The author is favorably disposed toward the Spanish *comedia*, giving it credit for inspiring Rotrou, Boisrobert, Cyrano, Montfleury, Corneille, and Molière. The absence of an index makes this work less useful than it should be. No bibliography.

[39]   Erickson, Martin E. "A Review of Scholarship with the Problem of a Spanish Source for *Love's Cure*," in *Studies in Comparative Literature*, Waldo F. McNeir, editor. Baton Rouge: Louisiana State University Press, 1962.

An enlightening study of the problems attendant upon pinning down sources and identifying borrowings, useful for the understanding of the methodology of literary criticism.

[40]   Farinelli, Arturo. *Divagaciones Hispánicas: Discursos y estudios críticos.* 2 vols. Barcelona: Imprenta Claraso, 1897, 1901.

Vol. I contains the essay "España y su literatura en el extranjero" in which Farinelli, famous Italian Hispanist, makes no claim for Spanish influence above the Italian in France but points out, however, the factors that give Spanish literature its special qualities which invite imitation.

Vol. II contains "España y Francia," a historical survey which traces the interest of French writers in Spanish material and notes that, in spite of this centuries-long interest, the first serious French study of Spain was in 1888. The author dates the beginning of Spanish influence from the 1543 translation of the *Amadís* into French. This volume also contains "John Lyly, Guevara y el 'eufuismo' en Inglaterra," in which Farinelli declares that the root of this "infección, la corrupción del gusto" should be sought in Italy, not in Spain, and challenges the critics who would blame Spain. He makes a convincing case, documenting it well. Copious notes are found all through these essays, which are valuable for their scholarship and readability. The work contains a bibliography of the literary relations of Spain with various other countries.

[41]   ———. *Ensayos y discursos de crítica literaria hispano-europea.* 2 vols. Rome: Fratelli Treves de Roma, [1926?].

Vol. II, pp. 326–344, treats of the literary relations of Spain and France during the Spanish Golden Age. One interesting note made by the author is that Tirso de Molina's play, *La celosa de sí misma* was translated into French by Boisrobert in 1649 as *La jalouse d'elle-même.* Farinelli provides plentiful bibliographical footnotes but an index to this study is lacking. Complete table of contents at front of Vol. I.

[42]   Farnham, Anthony E. "Saint Teresa and the Coy Mistress." ("Boston University Studies in English," No. 2, pp. 226–239.) Boston: Boston University Press, 1956.

The author contrasts Andrew Marvell's "To His Coy Mistress" and Crashaw's poem "A Hymn to the Name and Honor of the Admirable Saint Teresa," finding the antitheses emphasized by the poets' use of identical verse form, even though one poet is representing human love while the other seeks to express his reverence for the saintly figure of the Spanish mystic. Farnham develops his theme of contrasts and comparisons by close interpretation of texts, including both ideas and linguistic structures.

[43]   Flores, Angel, and M. J. Benardete, editors. *Cervantes Across the Centuries.* New York: The Dryden Press, 1947.

A group of essays which includes "Cervantes and English Literature" by Edwin B. Knowles (entry 75), in which the author analyzes English interpretations of *Don Quijote,* and "Translations of Cervantes into French" by Esther J. Crooks (entry 33), which considers *Don Quijote* in the light of French interpretations and translations and shows that interest in the Spanish work waned as Spain's political power declined.

[44] Flores, Robert M. "Sancho Panza through Three Centuries." Unpublished Master's thesis, University of Oregon, 1966.

Flores characterizes his study as "a survey of Sancho Panza's fortune through three and a half centuries of criticism, commentaries, imitations, and creations," noting the seventeenth- and eighteenth-century interpretation of Sancho as a buffoon, an attitude which was changed in the nineteenth century when the Romantics emphasized his wistfulness. Flores sees Sancho as the prototype for many "inspired clowns" in literature and provides quotations from Spanish, French, and English works that contain echoes of Sancho Panza's role in *Don Quijote*.

[45] Forsyth, Elliott. *La Tragédie Française de Jodelle à Corneille (1553–1640): Le Thème de la Vengeance*. (Publié avec le concours du Centre National de la Recherche Scientifique.) Paris: A. G. Nizet, 1962.

"La vengeance dans les traditions espagnoles," chapter IV, part 2, pp. 131–135, considers Spanish ideas of vengeance in relation to their literary and personal impact upon France, especially through the works of Lope de Vega, Calderón, and Tirso de Molina. Forsyth notes the influence of Guillén de Castro's *Las Mocedades del Cid* on Corneille on pp. 389–391 and 408–409, seeing Corneille elevate the Spanish idea of honor to become "un idéal plus élevé, plus intime, plus exigeant, que Corneille appelle sa 'gloire.'" Forsyth's well-organized and thorough study contains an extensive bibliography, an appendix which contains French tragedies written before 1640, and an index.

[46] Foulché-Delbosc, R. *Cervantes: "Le Licencié vidriera."* Nouvelle traduite en français avec un préface et des notes par R. Foulché-Delbosc. Paris: Librairie H. Welter, 1892.

The preface to this work is valuable for its historical material on Cervantes' *Novelas ejemplares*. The author gives an inventory of the French translations published from 1618 to 1891, describes the twenty-six he has looked at, gives biographical information concerning the translators of these works, and includes a criticism of the translations.

[47] Friederich, Werner P., and David Henry Malone. *Outline of Comparative Literature, from Dante Alighieri to Eugene O'Neill.* Chapel Hill: University of North Carolina Press, 1954.

"The Contributions of Spain," pp. 107–125, provides a rapid but valuable survey of Spain's literary achievements during the Golden Age (the authors present the varying views as to the dates of this age) and their impact upon the other countries of Western Europe. After a brief introduction the material is presented under the headings, "The Picaresque Novel," "Cervantes," "Spanish Mysticism," "The Spanish Comedia," "Lope de Vega," "The Cid," "Don Juan," "Calderón," and "Minor Spanish Contributions." The work is indexed, but no bibliography is provided.

[48] Gaselee, Stephen. "The Spanish Books in the Library of Samuel Pepys," in *Transactions of the Bibliographical Society,* Supplement 2. Oxford, 1921.

This is not a comparative study per se, but it may be of interest to researchers in Spanish-English literary history as an indication of the preferences in reading material of the day. Gaselee lists 185 Spanish books owned by Pepys, the list preceded by an introduction which states that Pepys was a competent Spanish scholar quite early in life, although he also read some Spanish books in French translations. Spanish words are often intercalated within his *Diary,* and the diarist was especially interested in collecting specimens of popular Spanish literature. His library of these books is now is the Pepysian Library at Magdalene College, Cambridge.

[49] Genouy, Hector. *L' "Arcadia" de Sidney dans ses rapports avec l' "Arcadia" de Sannazaro et la "Diana" de Montemayor.* Paris: Didier et Cie, 1928.

An examination of the extent to which Sidney was influenced by the Spanish pastorals and of how he transformed his borrowings to fashion a unique work. R. W. Zandwoort, in his review of this book in *RLC*, X (1930), praises the author for his astute literary criticism and for delving further than a surface analysis of sources, but he also brings him to task for not being aware of other recent scholarship on the subject.

[50]   ———. *L'Élément pastoral dans la poésie narrative et le drame en Angleterre de 1579–1640.* Paris: Henri Didier, 1928.

A thorough investigation into the English pastoral theme which also takes into account briefly the influence of other nations. The Spanish influence is found under "Influence espagnole et francaise," pp. 20–24, and under "Le drame italien et autres influences," pp. 333–343. An index would have helped the student greatly, since there are scattered references to Spanish literature throughout. A bibliography and notes are included.

[51]   González Ruiz, Nicolás. *Dos Genios contemporáneos, Cervantes y Shakespeare.* Barcelona: Editorial Cervantes, 1945.

Remarking that "Miguel de Cervantes y Guillermo Shakespeare representan la cumbre de la novela y la cumbre de la poesía dramática del mundo," the author finds bases for a parallel study of the two writers, including the idea that "Cervantes es el *Quijote* y las *Novelas ejemplares* como Shakespeare es *Macbeth* et *El Rey Lear*." An index would have made this study more helpful.

[52]   Gosse, Edmund. "Richard Crashaw," in *Seventeenth Century Studies.* London: William Heinemann, 1914.

Gosse gives credit to the Spanish mystics for setting Crashaw in motion, just as they did Friedrich von Spee in Germany. He calls Crashaw "an adept in every refinement of metrical structure which had been invented by the poet-artists of England, Spain, and Italy," and remarks that he sees the influence of Góngora in Crashaw's poetry. It is Gosse's opinion that "the progress of our poetical literature of the seventeenth century will never be thoroughly explained until some competent scholar shall examine the influence of Spanish poetry on our own."

[53] Gruber, Vivian Mercer. "François Rabelais and Miguel Cervantes, Novelists of Transition." Unpublished Ph.D. dissertation, Florida State University, 1960.

The author compares Rabelais's *Gargantua* and *Pantagruel* and *Don Quijote* on the basis of their being representative of the transitional epochs of the lifetimes of their authors. She contends that the French work represents the moment of transition from the Middle Ages to the Renaissance, while the Spanish novel represents the change from the Renaissance (including the Reformation and Counter-Reformation) to the modern period. In her contrast of the two authors Miss Gruber finds characteristic the excesses of Rabelais and the restraint of Cervantes, the skepticism of the French writer, and the Christian optimism of the Spaniard. Comparable, she believes, are their works, in that each began as a parody of an existing tradition and deepened in meaning so that each became didactic in addition to being entertaining. (Abstract appears in *DA*, XXI [1961], 2294.)

[54] Hainsworth, George. *Les "Novelas exemplares" de Cervantes en France au XVIIᵉ siècle; contribution à l'étude de la nouvelle en France*. Paris: H. Champion, 1933.

Hainsworth's study is scholarly and readable. Giving credit to Cervantes for providing new models which would contain the germ of the modern novel, the author remarks, "Grâce à Cervantes, la nouvelle française contient donc en germe toute une branche de la nouvelle moderne." This work is reviewed in *RLC*, XIV (1934), by Maurice Bardon, who calls it "une contribution des plus remarquables à l'histoire de Cervantes et de l'influence espagnole dans notre pays." Contains textual notes, index, and excellent bibliography.

[55] Hallam, Henry. *Introduction to the Literature of Europe in the Fifteenth, Sixteenth, and Seventeenth Centuries*. 2 vols. New York: Harper and Brothers, 1868.

This classic work contains a few references to the comparative aspects of literature during this period which may be useful; e.g., Vol. I, p. 209, the influence of Antonio de Guevara on English literature; Vol. II, pp. 389–391, the influence of the Spanish pastoral and the picaresque literature on English works. Although this book now is more than a century old, its background material on history is detailed and is presented in its international implications. Analyses of writings in all fields are presented.

[56] Hannay, David. *The Later Renaissance.* (Periods of European Literature, George Saintsbury, editor) New York: Charles Scribner's Sons, 1898.

The author analyzes the Later Renaissance (which in Spain he states began with *La Celestina*) by means of separate considerations of Spanish, English, and French literatures. The Spanish section includes some attention to historians and mystics, since their influence was diffused into the other countries. Hannay comments frequently on national influences and relationships, but these are difficult to locate quickly, since the index is scanty, consisting only of a list of authors.

[57] Harrison, T. P. Jr. *A Source of Sidney's "Arcadia."* ("Texas Studies in English," No. 6, pp. 53–71.) Austin: University of Texas Press, 1926.

Noting that some scholars have thought the Greek romances to be the principal sources for the *Arcadia*, Harrison states that Sidney knew these romances second hand through Montemayor's pastoral, which shows a decided Greek influence. Harrison's study then has as purpose "to point out the extent to which Sidney is indebted to the *Diana* for pastoral features and for some details of structure, technical devices, and plots." He does this systematically, using quotations from the English and the Spanish with accompanying commentaries.

[58] ———. *Googe's "Eglogs" and Montemayor's "Diana."* (Texas Studies in English," No. 5, pp. 68–78.) Austin: University of Texas Press, 1925.

Remarking that to Barnabe Googe belongs the honor of introducing the *Diana* into England, Harrison shows how Googe wove material from the Spanish pastoral into eclogues which contain the first traces of the *Diana* in English literature. Googe's work *Eglogs, Epytaphes, and Sonnetes* also contains the only lines of Spanish verse translated into English during the sixteenth century, those on bird-snaring by Garcilaso de la Vega. An interesting note, as Harrison points out, is that Googe sojourned in Ireland with Geoffrey Fenton and Edmund Spenser, an event which may indicate a connection between Spanish pastorals and Spenser's *Shepheardes Calender* through the influence of Googe on Spenser. Harrison rounds out his informative study with several comparisons of excerpts from the *Diana* and from Googe's eclogues.

[59] ———. *Shakespeare and Montemayor's "Diana."* ("Texas Studies in English," No. 6, pp. 72–120.) Austin: University of Texas Press, 1926.

It is the author's opinion that Shakespeare may have been more familiar with the *Diana* than is generally assumed. He sees its probable influence in *Two Gentlemen of Verona*, *A Midsummer Night's Dream*, and *Twelfth Night*, averring that Shakespeare could have read Montemayor in Spanish, for the *Diana* was widely enjoyed in England in the original. Harrison discusses at length the three above-mentioned Shakespearian plays in relation to Montemayor's work, pointing out noteworthy resemblances for which quotations are furnished. He points out that Shakespeare both pictures and satirizes the pastoral life, thus revealing intimate knowledge of the pastoral literature.

[60] Hatzfeld, Helmut. *Estudios Literarios sobre mística española.* Madrid: Editorial Gredos, 1955.

Chapter III—"El estilo nacional en los símiles españoles y franceses." Hatzfeld concludes that in general the French mystics are more abstract and rationalistic in their descriptions of their experiences, the Spanish more profound.

Chapter V—"Mística femenina clásica en España y Francia." This detailed comparative study of the mysticism of Santa Teresa de Jésus and that of Marie de l'Incarnation considers the mystics' cultural backgrounds and individual lives.

This volume of essays contains both textual notes and index.

[61]   Hilton, Ronald. "A Fundamental Michelet Antithesis: North vs. South, France vs. Spain," in *Four Studies in Franco-Spanish Relations*. Toronto: The University of Press, 1943.

Hilton takes note of the French historian's prejudiced attitude toward Spanish culture and his interpretation of the Inquisition as representing the essential qualities of Spanish thought, which Michelet considered poisonous to French culture. Hilton seeks to correct the misapprehensions created by Michelet's espousal of the "leyenda negra." This essay has merit for both historians and students of literature.

[62]   Hobbs, Edna Earle. "Spanish Influence on Plays of Beaumont and Fletcher." Unpublished Ph.D. dissertation, Florida State University, 1963.

Miss Hobbs considers fifty-two plays written by Beaumont and Fletcher and their collaborators, principally Massinger. She shows the intensive and extensive use these writers made of Spanish sources, especially of Cervantes. This work, which is organized according to author and play, gives attention not only to theme, plot, and incident, but also to language and character types. Proof is offered that Fletcher used untranslated novels of Salas Barbadillo for one of the plots of *Rule a Wife and Have a Wife*. (Abstract appears in *DA*, XXIV [1963], 283 f.)

[63]   *Hommage à Ernest Martinenche, études hispaniques et américaines*. Paris: Editions d'Artrey, 1939.

A collection of essays which includes two concerned with Golden Age influences: "Les trois poèmes de Crashaw sur Sainte-Thérèse," by Marcel Carayon (see entry 182), and "El Don Juan de Tirso y el de Molière como personajes barrocos," by Américo Castro (see entry 21). In the first the author sees the influence of Saint Teresa as crucial in the development of Richard Crashaw's thought; in the second Castro makes an analysis of the baroque style.

[64]   Hudson, Herman Cleophus. "The Development of Dramatic Criticism in England and Spain during the Elizabethan Period and the Golden Age." Unpublished Ph.D. dissertation, University of Michigan, 1962.

The author sees the dramatic criticism in both countries

following substantially the same course toward recognizing classical precepts, finding "remarkable similarity in attitudes and language which characterized the treatment of the issues involved." Hudson notes a trend toward the recognition of pleasure as a basic function of drama, with Spanish emphasis on the imaginative and the English on the rational. (Abstract appears in *DA*, XXIII [1962], 235.)

[65]   Hume, Martin. *Spanish Influence on English Literature*. London: E. Nash, 1905, 1964.

Long a standard work in the field of Spanish-English literary relations, but one that must be used in conjunction with other works. Hume traces the influences of the various genres of Spanish literature upon the literature of England. Chapters V and X deal with the Golden Age. A selective bibliography is included, but documentation is lacking. The 1964 edition is unrevised. Edwin B. Knowles, in his essay on Cervantes and English literature (q. v.), characterizes Hume's treatment of Cervantes as "often unsound."

[66]   Huszár, Guillaume (Vilmos). *L'Influence de l'Espagne sur le théâtre français des XVIIIᵉ et XIXᵉ siècles*. Paris: Librairie Honoré Champion, 1912.

Chapter I deals with "le génie espagnol"; the section on the eighteenth century (pp. 49–104) is organized around three playwrights, Lesage, Marivaux, and Beaumarchais, in their relation to Spain, with an analysis of their drama from the point of view of Spanish influence. In many cases, however, Huszár can call only upon his own strong intuition that the Spanish influence is present. This work is made less useful by the lack of an index.

[67]   ———. *Molière et l'Espagne*. Paris: H. Champion, 1907.

The author seeks to include all aspects of Molière's dependence upon the Spanish *comedia* for inspiration and for more tangible benefits. This work is organized into five sections: (1) Molière et la critique comparée; (2) Rapports de l'oeuvre de Molière avec la littérature espagnole; (3) Les comédies de Molière au point de vue de l'influence espagnole; (4) La comédie de Molière et le théâtre espagnole; and (5) La signification de l'oeuvre de Molière au point de vue de l'oeuvre littéraire européenne. This is a highly detailed work which is written with appreciation of the virtues of the traditional dramas of Spain and France as well as those of England and the classical era. Use of this study, however, is made difficult by the lack of an index. Bibliographical notes accompany the text.

[68]   ———. *Pierre Corneille et le théâtre espagnol.* Paris: E. Bouillon, 1903.

Huszár states his conviction that because he is Hungarian he can take a more objective point of view regarding the development of the French drama. His work seems to bear this out, as he carefully presents the contrasts and similarities of the Spanish and French dramas and by explication and example shows how the various elements were synthesized by Corneille, whose chief Spanish models Huszár sees as being Lope de Vega, Calderón, Castro, and Alarcón. Textual notes are provided, but the lack of an index is disconcerting. A favorable review by Brunetière may be found in *RDM* (1903).

[69]   Janelle, Pierre. *Robert Southwell, the Writer, a Study in Religious Inspiration.* London: Sheed and Ward, 1935.

Most of Janelle's study is concerned with French influences upon this English poet, but there are some interesting references to Spanish mystics, for these were a source of inspiration to Southwell, especially Diego de Estella.

[70]   Juderías, Julián. *La Leyenda negra.* Barcelona: Casa Editorial Araluce, 1917; Madrid: Editora Nacional, 1967.

A comprehensive work dealing with all aspects of the "leyenda negra," including the international aspect. Of especial interest to comparative students are "La España de los siglos XVI y XVII: la literatura," pp. 118–150, which shows how the culture of Spain was diffused throughout Western Europe through its superior works of literature, and "La España novelesca y fantástica," pp. 197–260, which describes the ideas of Spain and the Spanish people as they are delineated in the writings of non-Hispanic authors.

[71] Juretschke, Hans. *España ante Francia*. Madrid: Editorial Nacional, 1940.

There is no separate treatment of the sixteenth and seventeenth centuries in this study; therefore it will be necessary to consult the index for scattered references to this period. Bibliographical footnotes provide useful information for further research; a bibliography is included at the end of the volume.

[72] Kane, Elisha K. *Gongorism and the Golden Age; A Study of Exuberance and Unrestraint in the Arts.* Chapel Hill: University of North Carolina Press, 1928.

Kane examines the meaning, extent, qualities, predecessors, exponents, and literature of Gongorism. Material on the influence of Gongorism on the literatures (especially in poetry) of England and France may be found on pages 146–168. Ronsard and Lyly are noted at length.

[73] Ker, William Paton. "Cervantes, Shakespeare, and the Pastoral Idea," in *Form and Style in Poetry*. London: Macmillan and Co., Ltd., 1928.

Ker believes that England and Spain in "the great age" seem to have had a common understanding of many things. He cites the Spanish *arte mayor* as resembling the English "trick" of the heroic couplet used as a tag at the end of a blank verse tirade, common to Lope de Vega and Shakespeare. Ker notes, also, Cervantes' resemblance to Sir Philip Sidney, especially in connection with the dialogue on romance and drama at the end of Part I of *Don Quijote*, and finds similarities in Cervantes' story of Preciosa in the *Novelas ejemplares* and Shakespeare's *As You Like It*.

[74] ———. *Collected Essays*. Edited with an introduction by Charles Whibley. 2 vols. London: Macmillan and Co., Ltd., 1925.

Vol. II—"Spanish and English Ballads." An essay in conversational style based on a paper read to the Anglo-Spanish Society in King's College, London, June 14, 1918. Ker speculates about the spiritual ties of Spanish and English ballad makers, commenting, "Many things in their history seem to indicate a sort of unconscious resemblance."

[75]   Knowles, Edwin B. "Cervantes and English Literature," in *Cervantes Across the Centuries*, Angel Flores and M. J. Benardete, editors. New York: The Dryden Press, 1947.

Knowles sees four "relatively distinct" English interpretations of *Don Quijote* through the years: (1) seventeenth century—a farce; (2) eighteenth century—a serious satire; (3) nineteenth century—a work with spiritual implications; and (4) twentieth century—a "richly complex" work. Knowles points out that Coleridge was the first to make a sound interpretation of Don Quijote and Sancho Panza.

[76]   ———. *Four Articles on "Don Quixote" in England: Selections from Ph.D. Thesis*. New York. New York University Press, 1939.

This collection is composed of the following essays: (1) "*Don Quixote* in England before 1660"; (2) "Allusions to *Don Quixote* before 1660"; (3) "First and Second Editions of Shelton's *Don Quixote*, Part I, a Collation and Dating"; and (4) "*Don Quixote* through English Eyes." Bibliographical footnotes are included.

[77]   Lancaster, H. Carrington. *Adventures of a Literary Historian*. Baltimore: Johns Hopkins Press, 1942.

This collection of essays contains several articles on Spanish literature already published in journals. (These essays appear in our entries for periodical articles.) Of comparative interest are: "Lope's *Peregrino*, Hardy, Rotrou, and Beys," "Don Juan in a French Play of 1630," "The Ultimate Source of Rotrou's *Venceslas* and of Rojas Zorrilla's *No hay ser padre siendo rey*," "Castillo Solórzano's *El celoso hasta la muerte* and Montfleury's *École des jaloux*," and "Calderón, Boursault, and Ravenscroft."

[78]   ———. *The Pre-Classical Period, 1610–1634*. Part I (in 2 volumes) of *The History of French Dramatic Literature in the Seventeenth Century*. Baltimore: Johns Hopkins Press, 1929.

Lancaster is not convinced that the Spanish influence on the French pastorals in this period was very great and states that the *Diana* is almost the only book that might have had much to do with the development of this genre in France.

He believes, too, that Rotrou was the only dramatist directly affected by Spanish models up to 1634. Since Lancaster gives greater credit to the Italian influence, the student of Spanish will find references scattered in many places in the index which, however, is a satisfactory one.

[79]   ———. *The Period of Corneille, 1635–1651.* Part II (in 2 volumes) of *The History of French Dramatic Literature in the Seventeenth Century.* Baltimore: Johns Hopkins Press; London: Humphrey Milford, 1932.

It will be necessary to use the index for explicit references to Spanish influences. Lancaster, though he does not expand the Spanish contribution, does give it due consideration. He states that the vogue of the Spanish *comedia* began with D'Ouville, who had lived in Spain and who knew the works of Lope, Tirso, Calderón, and Montalván. His imitation of Spanish models was followed by Corneille, Brosse, and Scarron. This work is reviewed in *RLC*, XIII (1933), by L. Rivaille, who finds it "un instrument de travail précieux et presque indispensable à tous ceux qui voudraient avant d'étudier les pièces de quelque émule de Corneille, les situer dans leur temps." Lancaster's work contains also Part III, *The Age of Molière*, Part IV, *The Age of Racine*, and Part V, *Recapitulation.*

[80]   Lanson, Gustave. *Corneille.* Paris: Hachette, 1898.

Lanson states his theory that two equally legitimate types of tragedy existed in the French theater of Corneille's time— the drama of action and the psychological drama. He sees Corneille as being inspired by the example of the Spanish *comedia* and under this stimulus following his genius to perfect the psychological drama.

[81]   Lea, Henry Charles. *History of the Inquisition in Spain.* 4 vols. New York: The Macmillan Co.; London: Macmillan and Co., Ltd., 1906.

Lea's work is the standard account of the Inquisition in its many aspects, including its multiple influences upon the relations of Spain with other European countries, a knowledge of which is essential to the understanding of the literature of the times.

[82]   Lefranc, Abel. "Louis XIII, a-t-il appris l'espagnol?" in *Mélanges d'histoire littéraire générale et comparée, offerts à Fernand Baldensperger*. 2 vols. Paris: Librairie Ancienne Honoré Champion, 1930.

Vol. II, pp. 37–44—Lefranc points out that during the reign of Louis XIII the study and use of Spanish was so greatly encouraged and favored that it became one of the marks of "un honnête homme," chiefly because of the marriage of the King to Anne of Austria, daughter of Philip III. Lefranc examines briefly the careers of Ambrosio de Salazar and César Oudin, both teachers of Spanish at the court, and notes their intense rivalry. He commends Morel-Fatio's study of Ambrosio de Salazar (see entry 106) in this connection.

[83]   Lewis, Wyndam. *The Lion and the Fox: The Role of the Hero in the Plays of Shakespeare*. New York: Harper and Bros., n.d. (New York: Barnes & Noble, 1966, paper.)

Part VI (pp. 201–227), "The Two Knights," is a comparison of Don Quijote and Falstaff in Shakespeare's *Henry IV*, by which the author seeks to demonstrate the clash between medieval and Renaissance modes of thought. Lewis' idea is thought-provoking, but he rarely comes to grips with it and leaves the reader wondering what are the analogies he is illustrating. He does, however, express the opinion that Cervantes is kinder to the simpleton (the lion) than Shakespeare is, for he finds the master-subject of Shakespeare's plays to be the "Machiavellian obsession of his time."

[84]   Lhuillier, Paul, translator. *Choix de romances mauresques*, Preface by R. Foulché-Delbosc. Paris: F. Lebègue, 1921.

In the preface to this collection of twenty-five Moorish stories Foulché explains that they were all composed in Spain by the Spanish poets from the fifteenth to the seventeenth centuries. The Moorish theme was very much in fashion in France in the middle of the seventeenth century, he states, principally because of the work of several women: Mlle de Scudéry, author of *Almahide, ou l'Esclave reine*, Mme de La Fayette, author of *Zayde*, Mlle de la Roche-Guilhem, translator of *Las Guerras civiles de Granada*, and Mme de Villedieu, author of *Les Aventures et galanteries grenadines*.

[85] Linsalata, Carmine Rocco. *Smollett's Hoax: "Don Quixote" in English*. Stanford, Calif.: Stanford University Press, 1956.

A study in depth of the centuries-long dispute over Smollett's method and sources for his translation which appeared in 1755. Linsalata here concludes that Smollett did not accomplish the translation of *Don Quijote* alone, for he knew no Spanish. Copious parallel passages from other contemporary translations are given by Linsalata to support his thesis.

[86] Lintilhac, Eugène François. *La Comédie, dix-septième siècle*. Vol. III of *Histoire générale du théâtre en France*. Paris: Ernest Flammarion, n.d.

Lintilhac includes a brief consideration of Spanish influences, pp. 70–78. He notes Corneille's debt to Spanish works, especially to Alarcón's *La Verdad sospechosa*.

[87] Liuima, P. Antanas. *Aux Sources du "Traité de l'amour de Dieu" de Saint François de Sales*. (Collectanea Spiritualia, Vol. V.) Rome: Université Grégorienne, 1959.

Liuima's monograph is a valuable addition to the criticism of the literature of mysticism in its international aspects. This literature has achieved new importance for those researching into the origins of metaphysical poetic ideas of the seventeenth century and their relation to modern poetry.

[88] Lyonnet, Henry. *"Le Cid" de Corneille*. Paris: Malfère, 1929.

A study of the external qualities of the play, including Spanish sources, which brings together much scholarship that has been done heretofore. The orientation is historical, not critical, but the student should check the accuracy of some of the statements (as that the French did not know much of Spanish literature in 1636) and dates. Contains a bibliography of works on the subject. Lyonnet's book is reviewed in *RHLF*, XXXVI (1929), by René Bray, who remarks that the author is not one of the "mieux informés" on the subject he has chosen to explicate.

[89]   McCann, Eleanor Margaret. "The Influences of 16th and 17th Century Spanish Mystics and Ascetics on Some Metaphysical Writers." Unpublished Ph.D. dissertation, Stanford University, 1953.

Miss McCann finds "indubitable borrowings" from the works of such Spanish mystics and ascetics as Juan de Valdés, Ignacio de Loyola, Luis de Granada, Diego de Estella, Santa Teresa, Juan de la Cruz, Luis de Léon, and Nieremberg by such English writers as Robert Southwell, John Donne, George Herbert, Richard Crashaw, Joseph Beaumont, and Henry Vaughn. The concept of oxymora found in Juan de la Cruz's analogy of cauterization, and in Luis de Léon's interpretation of Christ are presented as areas of borrowing. (Abstract appears in *DA*, XIII [1953], 229 f.)

[90]   McNeir, Waldo F., editor. *Studies in Comparative Literature.* Baton Rouge: Louisiana State University Press, 1962.

Included in this collection is an essay useful to students of comparative drama, "Parallel Tendencies in English and Spanish Tragedy in the Renaissance," by Jean Alexander (see entry 1). Miss Alexander sees the Spanish and English dramas as similar in orientation and use of dramatic devices. Also in this volume is Martin E. Erickson's "A Review of Scholarship with the Problem of a Spanish Source for *Love's Cure*" (see entry 39).

[91]   Madariaga, Salvador de. *Don Juan y La Don-Juanía.* Buenos Aires: Editorial Sudamericana, n.d.

Madariaga treats the comparative aspect of the Don Juan theme in a drama of his own, prefacing it with an essay which examines the international nature of the subject. The Don Juans of Tirso de Molina, Molière, Byron, Zorrilla, Mozart, and Pushkin appear as characters in the play, along with one female character.

[92]   ———. *Englishmen, Frenchmen, Spaniards: an Essay in Comparative Psychology.* London: Oxford University Press, 1928.

The author finds in the course of his analyses of these three nations that three keys can be devised by which one can explain the psychology of the people, for they constitute the "idea-sentiment-force" by which each nation lives. The keys are: England, fair play; France, *le droit*; Spain, *el honor*. Madariaga admits that these concepts are untranslatable; therefore he provides a thorough explanation of each, his objective being to dispel prejudice through understanding. The work is written with humor and excellent intentions, but his generalizations are too facile to be adequate for this complex subject. Nevertheless, they are not without value for aiding in the interpretation of the literatures of these nations.

[93] ————. "English Sidelights on Spanish Literature," in *Shelley and Calderón and Other Essays on English and Spanish Poetry*. London: Constable and Company, Ltd., 1920.

Madariaga finds spiritual affinities in the literatures of Spain and England based upon their realistic attitudes toward life. His comparisons are embodied in commentaries on the literatures as he follows them chronologically. In the Golden Age he juxtaposes Garcilaso de Vega and Sidney, Lope de Vega and Shakespeare, Calderón and Milton. He would, however, put only one English figure on the highest literary plane reached by Spain, the figure of Shakespeare.

[94] ————. *Ensayos anglo-españoles*. Madrid: Publicaciones Atenea, 1922.

"Paralelos anglo-españoles," pp. 145–190. In this essay Madariaga finds parallels between the English Renaissance drama and that of Golden Age Spain, concluding that they have in common what he calls "realismo." He comments, "Inglaterra y España son las dos únicas naciones modernas que han creado un teatro verdaderamente original, es decir, un teatro nacido del maridaje de la realidad con el genio nacional sin intervención de modelo clásico prejuicio o tradición. Este hecho bastaría para justificar el estudio comparativo de la literaturas inglesa y española como indispensable complemento de cada una de ellas." Madariaga does not develop the parallels he finds through example or analysis in this essay.

[95]   ———. *On Hamlet*. London: Hollis and Carter, 1948.

In this interpretation of Cervantes' and Shakespeare's characters Madariaga presents an analogy between Don Quijote and Hamlet: Hamlet represents the pressure of society on the individual, while Don Quijote represents the pressure of the individual on society.

[96]   Magendie, Maurice. *Du Nouveau sur "L'Astrée"*. Paris: H. Champion, 1927.

Magendie studies in great detail the historical and literary sources of *Astrée* by Honoré d'Urfé. He sees the *Diana* of Montemayor and Cervantes' *Galatea* as two important sources, among many others. Reviewed by H. C. Lancaster (*MLN*, 1928), who observes that Magendie should have been more cognizant of recent scholarship on d'Urfé's work before he published the results of his own investigation.

[97]   ———. *Le Roman français au XVIIᵉ siècle de "L'Astrée" au "Grand Cyrus"*. Paris: Librairie E. Droz, 1932.

The author's treatment of Spanish sources which stimulated the beginnings of the French novel may be found on pp. 52–67. Magendie gives credit to *Amadís de Gaula*, *Diana*, *Don Quijote*, and Tirso de Molina's *Los Cigarrales* (source for *Le Tolédan* and *Le Roman véritable*), noting that the Spanish *novelas*, translated into French, were much imitated. The *comedia* is seen as an influence on the French novel's development. This work, though of great interest, is rendered less useful because it has no index. Only a short "table de matières" is provided to guide the student.

[98]   Marsan, Jules. *La Pastorale dramatique en France à la fin du XVIᵉ et au commencement du XVIIᵉ siècle*. Paris: Hachette, 1905.

Marsan investigates the literary origins of the pastoral in Italy and Spain and traces it through its flourishing and decline in its international aspects: Chapter V, "Les influences étrangères et le tempérament français"; Chapter VI, "Hispanisme du seizième siècle." The work also includes a list of translations of Spanish pastoral poetry. The lack of index is disappointing. W. W. Grey, in his review of Marsan's work (*MLR*, 1906), praises the bibliography but finds the absence of an index "inexcusable."

[99]   Martinenche, Ernest. *La Comedia espagnole en France de Hardy à Racine.* Paris: Librairie Hachette et Cie, 1900.

A thorough study of the Spanish drama in relation to the use made of it by French writers as they borrowed from it, imitated it, and transformed it. Martinenche finds in the drama of the sixteenth and seventeenth centuries the image of an epoch, "le génie national lui-même, avec ses grandeurs et ses petitesses."

[100]   Mathews, Ernst G. "Studies in Anglo-Spanish Cultural and Literary Relations, 1598–1700." Unpublished Ph.D. dissertation, Harvard University, 1938.

Mathews divides his work into two parts, one dealing with the political milieu, one with the literary. In this latter part he analyzes the translations of the *Dianas* of Gerardo and of Spanish verse and weighs their value and influence. He notes the role of Aphra Behn in England for her popularizing of the *novela* through the use of Alonso de Castillo Solórzano's *El celoso hasta la muerte* (1630) for her comedy *The False Count* (1682). Mathews sees Montemayor's influence on Shakespeare in *Two Gentlemen of Verona*, as he also observes the effect of the works of Boscán, Garcilaso, Lope de Vega, and Góngora on English poetry. The study includes a list of English translations of Spanish works published during the seventeenth century which covers explorers' accounts, religious writings, works on nature, moral philosophy, as well as fiction. Mathews omits Cervantes and the picaresque novel from his work.

[101]   Matulka, Barbara. *The Cid as a Courtly Hero; from the "Amadís" to Corneille.* ("Columbia University Institute of French Studies," No. 3) New York: Columbia University Press, 1928.

Miss Matulka traces the evolution of the Cid theme, studying it in relation to knightly themes and motifs found in the *Amadís*, and seeing *Las Mocedades del Cid* as a junction of the Cid legend and the *Amadís* themes. The author concludes her delineation of the subject with a study of the *Cid-Amadís* theme in France before the time of Pierre Corneille.

[102] ———. *The Novels of Juan de Flores and Their European Diffusion.* ("New York University Centennial Series.") New York: New York University Press, 1931. (Also New York: Columbia University Institute of French Studies, 1931.)

Miss Matulka shows how the French and English translations of Juan de Flores' novels *Grisel y Mirabella* and *Grimalte y Gradissa* were influential upon the literature of the seventeenth century. *Grisel y Mirabella* is considered to be the source of Mlle de Scudéry's *Le Prince déguisé*; the French translation of *Grimalte y Gradissa* was made by the poet Maurice de Scève. In England the translation of the latter novel appeared in 1606; elements from it are found in Swetnam's *The Woman Hater*, Miss Matulka points out. A thoroughly worth-while monograph for comparative literature students interested in this period.

[103] Mazur, Oleh. "The Wild Man in the Spanish Renaissance and Golden Age Theatre, a Comparative Study." Unpublished Ph.D. dissertation, University of Pennsylvania, 1966.

In Part I of this study the author gives attention to the "wild man" as an evolving concept in Spain and other parts of Europe. He compares the Spanish "salvaje" and "wild man" in faraway places, observing how he is represented in art and literature, especially the English, French, Italian, and German drama. Part II shows the "wild man" as a dramatic device in Spain from 1530 to 1700. The impact of the American Indian is emphasized. The Spanish interpretations of the Indian were highly important, since they gave information to playwrights in the other nations. (Abstract appears in *DA*, XXIII-A [1966], 1341 f.)

[104] Menéndez y Pelayo, M. *Orígenes de la novela.* 4 vols. (Nueva Biblioteca de Autores Españoles, I, VI, XIV, XXI.) Madrid: Casa Editorial Bailly-Bailliere, S.A., 1925. 4 vols. (Edición nacional de las obras completas, XIII–XVI.) Santander: Aldus, 1943. 4 vols. (Edición nacional de las obras completas,

segunda edición, XIII–XVI.) Madrid: Consejo Superior de Investigaciones Científicas, 1963.

The 1925 edition contains an excellent treatment of the subject, but the work is difficult to use because of the lack of an index as well as the choice of Roman numerals for pagination. Comments on the relationships of Spanish works and authors to those of other nations are found throughout. Of especial interest are the following: Vol. I—Guevara, CCCL ff.; *Arcadia*, CD; *Diana* (influence on d'Urfé, Sidney, Shakespeare) CDXXXII f., CDXLII ff.; Antonio de Lofrasso, CDLXIII. Vol. II—"El Cuenta español en Francia" (at the time of Louis XIII), LXXXI–LXXXVI; Shakespeare and Spanish models, CXXXIII–CXXXVI. Vol. III—"*La Celestina* y su influjo en las literaturas extranjeras" (French and English), CXXXIII–CXXXVII.

The 1943 and 1963 editions are paginated with Arabic numerals and well indexed (at the end of Vol. IV) for the use of students of Spanish, but those in comparative literature will not find certain details included in the index. Therefore it will be necessary to peruse the volumes carefully to find passing references to the subject being researched.

[105]   Mimnaugh, Joan L. "The Tragic World in Lope de Vega's *El Mayordomo de la duquesa de Amalfi* and John Webster's *Duchess of Malfi*." Unpublished Master's thesis, University of Oregon, 1950.

Miss Mimnaugh finds the common source of these two dramas in the twenty-sixth *novella* of Mateo Bandello, an Italian writer, and compares the treatment accorded the theme by the other writers, Lope and Webster, seeing Webster's world as a truly tragic one, while Lope's world is one where justice triumphs. No comparative studies are in the author's bibliography.

[106]   Morel-Fatio, Alfred. *Ambrosio de Salazar et l'étude d'espagnol en France sous Louis XIII*. Paris: Picard; Toulouse: Privat, 1901.

A study of the career of Salazar, whose life was devoted to bringing knowledge of the then hated Spain to Frenchmen. Salazar's appointment as tutor to the King when the

royal marriage to the Infanta Anna of Spain was planned
encouraged him but also earned for him the enmity of such
men as César Oudin. Gustave Lanson, in his review of this
work in *RHL*, 1901, calls it "un modèle d'érudition précise
et sobre."

[107] ———. *Études sur l'Espagne.* 4 vols. Paris: Librairie E. Bouillon, 1895, 1904, 1906, 1925.

Material on subjects of comparative interest: Vol. I—
"L'Espagne en France," pp. 3–108. A general essay presenting information and opinions on Franco-Spanish politics,
literature, and travel. Vol. II—"Histoire de deux sonnets,"
pp. 141–146. This traces some early Italian, Spanish, and
French efforts to use the sonnet form, from Castiglione,
Mendoza, Espinosa, Lope de Vega, Scarron, Voiture, and
others less well known. Several examples are presented with
valuable critical remarks. Vol. IV—"L'espagnol, langue uni-
verselle," pp. 189–219. Stresses the importance of the Spanish language in French affairs during the sixteenth century,
beginning with 1536 when Charles V spoke in Spanish to
Pope Paul III at Rome in the presence of many nobles and
dignitaries. This interest declined with the separation of the
Empire. Also in Vol. IV will be found "Bernardino de Mendoza. 1. La vie. 2. Les oeuvres," pp. 373–490. A careful view
of Mendoza, author of the *Commentaries*, ambassador to
France, and visitor at the court of Elizabeth of England.

This work contains much good material for further research and is presented in a manner which indicates the
author's objectivity.

[108] ———. "L'Espagne du Don Quijote," in *Studies in European
Literature.* (Taylorian Lectures, 1889–1899.) Oxford: Clarendon Press, 1900.

The author comments that no nation has ever equaled
England in its appreciation of Cervantes and his works.
Noting, too, that "le cervantisme" took shape first in England, he gives credit to the Englishmen who have worked
to create this enthusiasm and goes on to show how *Don
Quijote* and other works reflect the Spain in which Cervantes
lived.

[109] ————. *La Comedia espagnole du XVII* *siècle*. Paris: Librairie Ancienne Honoré Champion, Édouard Champion, 1923.

Morel-Fatio is a severe critic of the *comedia*, finding it inferior to the dramas of France and England. The reason for this, he indicates, is the characteristic of impatience which he finds in the Spaniards—they can neither "finir ni polir," and they must always put a moral into their plays; moreover, they are superficial and do not truly teach anything. He admits, however, that the Spanish drama has enriched "le trésor commun" of European literature. This essay is well worth reading even though it is outdated and biased. It is reviewed in *MLR*, XX (1925), by William J. Entwistle, who finds it a "reasoned censure" of the *comedia*.

[110] Mottola, Anthony Clare. "The *Amadís de Gaula* in Spain and in France." Unpublished Ph.D. dissertation, Fordham University, 1962.

In the sixteenth and early seventeenth centuries the *Amadís*, adapted in the *Thresors*, served as a book of instruction in courtly grace and filled an important role as the model of the ideal knight and lady, concludes Mottola in this study. He attributes this success to the skillful efforts of Montalvo, the Spanish writer of the legend, and to Nicolas de Herberay, the French translator. (Abstract appears in *DA*, XXIII [1962], 1368 f.)

[111] Pastor, Antonio. *Breve historia de hispanismo inglés*. Madrid, 1948. (Originally published in *Arbor*, April–May 1948.)

A valuable survey of British scholarship done in the field of Hispanic studies up to 1948. Pastor's pamphlet is reviewed in *CL*, 1953, by Bernardo Gicovate, who comments that the author writes "this accurate and solid history of British Hispanism" with "intelligent penetration." Pastor notes the renewed modern English interest in Calderón and the concepts of the Counter-Reformation.

[112] ————. "Un Embajador de España en la escena inglesa," in *Homenaje ofrecido a Menéndez Pidal*, Vol. III. Madrid: Librería y Casa Editorial Hernando, S.A., 1925.

This study concerns the Spanish diplomat D. Diego Sarmiento de Acuña (later el conde de Gondomar), whose career formed the basis of the comedy *A Game at Chess*, by Thomas Middleton, which Pastor calls "la única comedia verdaderamente aristofanesca de la literatura inglesa." This play, says Pastor, expressed the opposition of the English people to the Spanish policies of King James I and ruined the popularity of Don Diego in England. Pastor's work includes an act-by-act summary of Middleton's play, identifying the characters as representatives of the major political figures of contemporary England and Spain.

[113]   Patchell, Mary Frances Corinne. *The Palmerin Romances in Elizabethan Prose Fiction.* ("Columbia University Studies in English and Comparative Literature," Vol. XIII, No. 166.) New York: Columbia University Press, 1947.

Miss Patchell describes the "peculiar characteristics" of the Spanish romance of chivalry and how these romances have contributed to the development of English fiction. She seeks to establish that this chivalric literature had a more extended influence in England than has hitherto been believed. The work is indexed, contains a lengthy bibliography, and has an appendix which provides summaries of the Palmerin romances.

[114]   Peers, E. Allison. "Juan Luis Vives and England," in *St. John of the Cross and Other Lectures and Addresses, 1920–1945.* London: Faber and Faber, Ltd., 1946.

Erasmus introduced the works of Vives to Thomas More, and under More's patronage Vives went to England in 1523, becoming the tutor to the future Queen Mary. Peers points out how influential Vives' works on pedagogy were in England, as they were admired by More and other humanists.

[115]   ———. *Spanish Mysticism: A Preliminary Survey.* 2 vols. London: Methuen & Co., Ltd., 1924.

Although this study concentrates upon the Spanish mysticism, the student will find references in the index to some French mystics, notably François de Sales, who read Spanish religious works and whose thinking was changed by them. Moreover, this work provides first-hand knowledge of some mystical writings which had influence upon John Donne and other English authors, for excerpts from the mystics' own writings are included, with analyses of the imagery employed by them in the description of their experiences. Each volume of this work is separately indexed.

[116] Pegues, Charles Melton. "Spanish Literature as Portrayed in the *Revue des deux mondes* (1829–1929)." Unpublished Master's thesis, University of Illinois, 1931.

Pegues analyzes the types of articles printed on Spanish literature in the French periodical during this period, articles written by such men as Prosper Mérimée, Théophile Gautier, Alfred Morel-Fatio, Ferdinand Brunetière, René Bazin, and José-María de Heredia, and comes to the conclusion that in their treatment of Spanish literature these French writers are both scholarly and sympathetic.

[117] Pierce, Frank. "Ercilla and England," in *Hispanic Studies in Honour of I. González Llubera.* Oxford: The Dolphin Book Co., Ltd. Printed in Spain by Tipografía Moderna, Valencia, 1959.

Ercilla, author of the *Araucana* (first published in 1569), was one of the "classics" of the Golden Age, Pierce points out. First mention of him in English is found in Minsheu's *Spanish Grammar* (1599). The *Araucana* increased in fame in the eighteenth century through the efforts of such men as William Hayley and Hugh Blair, whose work "created at least something like a connected interest in Spanish literature." Pierce notes that "Ercilla and his poem have, of course, survived well in Spain and France, but much less well in this country."

[118] Plaidy, Jean. *The Spanish Inquisition.* New York: The Citadel Press, 1967.

This volume describes the rise, growth, and end of the Spanish Inquisition, being a thorough study of this institution in all its facets, valuable for an understanding of Golden Age attitudes. Of especial interest is Chapter III, "The Inquisition in Some European Countries," pp. 42–65.

[119] Protzman, Merle I., editor. *"Les illustres fous" de Charles Beys.* Baltimore: Johns Hopkins Press, 1942.

In his critical introduction to this work Protzman considers the case for Lope de Vega's *El Peregrino en su patria* as a source for Beys' play and concludes that there are many similarities in plot, although it is not known whether Beys used the Spanish original or a French translation of Lope's work. Protzman draws upon scholarship already done on this subject, adding to the value of his comments, which in themselves are carefully done.

[120] Puibusque, Adolphe de. *Histoire comparée des littératures espagnole et française.* ("Ouvrage qui a remporté le prix proposé par l'Académie Française au concours extraordinaire de 1842.") 2 vols. Paris: G. A. Dentu, 1843.

In this work, which is used as a source by scholars even today, the Golden Age is treated from p. 24 of Vol. I to p. 336 of Vol. II. Included is a thorough discussion of milieu as well as literature; pp. 361–524 contain the author's remarks and biographical information concerning persons treated within the work. Copious notes are provided. In his review of Puibusque's book, Gustave Lanson, in *RHLF*, 1896, finds in this study "les affirmations arbitraires, les indications vagues; les erreurs, et les lacunes . . . y sont nombreuses."

[121] Pujals, Esteban, translator. *Las Novelas de caballerías españolas y portuguesas. Despertar de la novela caballeresca en la península ibérica y expansión e influencia en el extranjero.* Madrid: Consejo Superior de Investigaciones Científicas, 1952.

Spanish translation of Henry Thomas' *Spanish and Portuguese Romances of Chivalry* (see entry 142).

[122] Quijano Terán, Margarita. *"La Celestina" y "Otelo": Estudio de literatura dramática comparada.* ("Ediciones Filosofía y Letras," No. 15.) Mexico, D.F.: Universidad Nacional Autónoma de Mexico, 1957.

Miss Terán is of the opinion that Shakespeare's *Othello* contains many merits not found in *La Celestina*; she believes that the English dramatist has created characters of greater depth than the ones created by Rojas, whose characters she considers childish by comparison. She sees, too, the characters in *Othello* better motivated than their counterparts in the Spanish play. Miss Terán has included a selective bibliography which contains works of recent criticism on Shakespeare and *La Celestina*. Her study is reviewed in *SQ*, X (1959), by John Leon Lievsay, who thinks it generally good but weak in the criticism of Rojas' drama.

[123] Quilter, Daniel Edward. "The Image of the *Quijote* in the Seventeenth Century." Unpublished Ph.D. dissertation, University of Illinois, 1962.

Part I of Quilter's study consists of an analytic review of information gathered by many Cervantine scholars in Spain; Part II, chapters 6 and 7 contain a synthesis of numerous recent studies on Cervantes in France and England, with a comparative study of the popularity of works translated from the Spanish. (Abstract appears in *DA*, XXIII [1963], 4363 f.)

[124] Randall, Dale B. J. *The Golden Tapestry: A Critical Survey of Non-chivalric Spanish Fiction in English Translation, 1543–1657*. Durham, N.C.: Duke University Press, 1963.

Randall states his purpose as being to make "a synthesis to clarify the over-all Spanish contribution" to the English literary reservoir and to "suggest the nature and extent of the Spanish fiction—especially the non-chivalric, that was imported for Renaissance English readers." Chapter VIII contains a statistical analysis of translations with their dates. An index is provided, but bibliography is found only within the context of the footnotes, a disadvantage which the author anticipates and explains by saying that he could not possibly hope to record all his debts. The student, however, would probably have benefited if the bibliography had been included. A generally favorable review by Joan Pierson is found in *CL*, XVI (1964).

[125] Reese, Lowell Grant. "Lope de Vega and Shakespeare: A Comparative Study of Tragicomic Style." Unpublished Ph.D. dissertation, University of Washington, 1962.

Reese reviews tragicomic theories from classical times on, including medieval Christian drama, with an analysis of the structure of Shakespeare's *As You Like It* and *Othello* to show how the structural elements blend in one of Shake-speare's last plays, *The Winter's Tale*, and with a similar analysis of Lope de Vega's *La Dama boba, El Castigo sin venganza, and Peribáñez y el Comendador de Ocaña*. Reese concludes that each playwright comes to treat a "fuller reality" in his last-named play, in contrast to the "partial reality" found in the other plays. (Abstract appears in *DA*, XXIV [1963], 285 f.)

[126]   Revillout, C. J. *Beaumarchais et la comédie espagnole*. Montpel-lier: Imprimerie de Gras, 1867.

Originally a lecture, this short essay gives the details of Beaumarchais's visit to Spain in 1764 as recounted by Clavijo. The result of the visit, Revillout remarks, was the awakening of Beaumarchais's talent for comedy. (Subtitle: "Conférence faite à l'ancienne loge de mer de Perpignan le 15 février, 1867.")

[127]   Reynier, Gustave. *"Le Cid" de Corneille*. Paris: Mellottée, 1929.

In his usual thorough manner Reynier makes an investi-gation of Corneille's use of Guillén de Castro's *Las Moce-dades del Cid* in the construction of his own drama upon this legendary Spanish figure.

[128]   ———. *Le Roman réaliste au XVIIᵉ siècle*. Paris: Librairie Hachette, 1914.

Reynier begins his study of the realistic novel in France with a consideration of the development of the Spanish picaresque story, commencing with the *Lazarillo* in 1554. Pp. 1–84 contain this introductory material.

[129]   ———. *Le Roman sentimental avant "L'Astrée."* Paris: Colin et Cie, 1908.

Reynier divides his work into two parts: Part I traces the origins of this genre in Spain, Italy, and France; Part II is entitled " Le Roman sentimental à la fin du XVIᵉ et au com-mencement du XVIIᵉ siècles jusqu'à l'*Astrée*." The author sees the pastoral movement related to the state of society and customs during and after the civil wars as this period of strife encouraged a sad and serious view of love. This is a valuable and useful work with a good bibliography of the "roman sentimental," and it is indexed.

[130]   ————. *Thomas Corneille, sa vie et son théâtre.* Paris: Hachette et Cie, 1892.

Reynier brings up to this date the study of the imitation of the Spanish theater in France, drawing upon the work of Roy on Sorel, and of Morillot, Person, Vianey, Steffens, and Stiefel on Rotrou and Scarron. A useful work for the student of literary history.

[131]   Riddle, Lawrence M. *The Genesis and Sources of Pierre Corneille's Tragedies from "Medée" to "Pertharite."* ("Johns Hopkins Studies in Romance Literatures and Languages," No. 3.) Baltimore: Johns Hopkins Press, 1926.

A painstaking study in depth of Corneille's sources, found in the contemporary French, Spanish, and Italian theater. Although this is a well-studied area in literary relations, Riddle has presented a meritorious work which sheds new light on Corneille's methods as he transformed his borrowed gleanings.

[132]   Rivet, Mother Mary M. *The Influence of the Spanish Mystics on the Works of Saint François de Sales.* Washington: Catholic University of America Press, 1941.

A detailed comparison of the French mystic with the Spanish Fray Luis de Granada, Saint Ignatius, and Saint Teresa. Excerpts from the texts of these mystics are used to illustrate the writer's conclusions. A review of this work by N. Chédid can be found in *LLR*, 1949. The reviewer calls it a nonexhaustive study but conscientiously done and useful to one who wishes knowledge of this subject. He regrets the omission of Diego de Estella, however.

[133]   Schelling, Felix E. *Foreign Influences in Elizabethan Plays.* New York and London: Harper and Bros., 1923.

The influence of Spanish literature on Fletcher and other playwrights is treated, pp. 109–127. In general Schelling says of Spanish influences, "Spanish literary influences on the drama in Tudor times were slight and confined, almost entirely, to an occasional plot. . . . In the reign of James, Beaumont and Fletcher, Massinger, and William Rowley . . . drew on Spanish sources. . . . In the reign of Charles . . . the Spanish drama for the first time came in touch with the English stage . . . was closest at the Restoration . . . but was soon eclipsed by that of France." Schelling considers various plays to find their similarities to Spanish models.

[134] Schneer, Richard J. "Juan Huarte de San Juan and His *Examen de Ingenios,* a Sixteenth Century Spanish Contribution to Education." Unpublished Ph.D. dissertation, New York University, 1961.

Commenting that "Spain's non-literary contribution to world culture is relatively neglected," the author studies the life and works of Juan Huarte to bring to American scholars' attention how advanced were the thought and methodology of this Spaniard in regard to educational problems. Useful for study in conjunction with works on Juan Luis Vives, who was so influential in England. (Abstract appears in *DA,* XXII [1961], 567.)

[135] Sedwick, Frank. *A History of the Useless Precaution Plot in Spanish and French Literature.* ("University of North Carolina Studies," No. 49.) Chapel Hill: University of North Carolina Press, 1964.

A thorough treatment of the theme of male protectors of female virtue who are deceived by the waywardness of their charges. Sedwick, after a short history of the theme in earlier Western literature, traces its development in the works of Cervantes, Zayas, Scarron, Lope de Vega, Moreto, Molière, and others. Specific plays considered are those from the sixteenth century to the early nineteenth century, when the theme died. A chart which graphically identifies the presence or absence of characteristics of this theme in the dramas is included. This work, carefully done throughout, has a bibliography and textual notes.

[136] Segall, Jacob Bernard. *Corneille and the Spanish Drama.* New York: Columbia University Press, Macmillan Company, agents, 1902; New York: Ams Press, 1966.

The main comparisons found in this study are between Castro's *Las Mocedades del Cid* and *Le Cid* of Corneille, and between *La Verdad sospechosa* of Alarcón and Corneille's *Le Menteur*. Some attention is given to the Spanish influence on Corneille's *L'Illusion, La Suite du Menteur, Héraclius,* and *Don Sanche d'Aragon*. Segall, however, emphasizes Corneille's originality in his unique method of presentation which minimizes the similarities to his models. This study includes detailed plot summaries and comparative quotations from the plays. No index is provided.

[137] Seillière, Ernest. *Les origines romanesques de la morale et de la politique romantiques.* Paris: Renaissance du Livre, 1920.
Seillière sees the novel as a sort of romantic encyclopedia, summing up the history of chivalric, courtly, and Platonic eroticism in Europe as he examines the last stage of the development in the seventeenth century which completed the deification of women. He finds the sources of *L'Astrée*, the influential French romance, in Spain and in Italy.

[138] Simonde de Sismondi, J. C. L. *De la Littérature du midi de l'Europe.* Paris, 1813.
This work is a pioneer one in the field of Spanish-French literary criticism, one which E. Allison Peers commends as being "el primero en subrayar, en francés, el dualismo del *Quijote* que la crítica de los siglos sucesivos iba a poner más y más de relieve." Instead of being a jestbook, as it was considered to be in the early years of its history, Sismondi points out, *Don Quijote* is in reality "un libro triste." (See Peers' article, "Aportación de los Hispanistas extranjeros al estudio de Cervantes," entry 303).

[139] Sorkin, Max. *Paul Scarron's Adaptations of the Comedia.* New York: Appellate Law Printers, Inc., 1938.
Sorkin takes note of the Spanish influence on Scarron and others in a short section entitled, "Spanish Influence on French Comedy of the XVIIth Century," pp. 6–8, remarking, "It is from 1639 to 1658 that the influence of the Spanish 'comedia' is felt with increasing force." He points to the principal French authors concerned with the imitation of the *comedia* as D'Ouville, Pierre Corneille, Scarron, Thomas

Corneille, and Boisrobert. Sorkin gives credit to D'Ouville for introducing Calderón into France and to Scarron for importing Castillo Solórzano and Rojas. He notes, however, that Scarron did not imitate Spanish models slavishly but asserted his independence in characterization and technical structure, adding that Scarron's success as a dramatist was a powerful factor in keeping alive the vogue of the Spanish *comedia*.

[140] Thomas, Henry. "Shakespeare and Spain," in *Studies in European Literature*. (The Taylorian Lectures, Second Series, 1920–30.) Oxford: Clarendon Press, 1930.

Thomas' theme is Spain's influence as shown in Shakespeare's works, although he admits that this provable influence is small. He disapproves of a statement by Aubrey Bell that Shakespeare seems to have known Spanish well: it is his opinion that evidence for this is lacking. Nevertheless, he does not hesitate to characterize the Spanish romances of chivalry, especially the *Amadís*, and the *Diana* as works whose influence may be detected in Shakespeare's drama.

[141] ———. "Shakespeare y España," in *Homenaje ofrecido a Menéndez Pidal*, Vol. I. Madrid: Librería y Casa Editorial Hernando (S.A.), 1925.

This is the article which formed the basis of Thomas' Taylorian lecture (see above) given at Oxford.

[142] ———. *Spanish and Portuguese Romances of Chivalry: The Revival of the Romance of Chivalry in the Spanish Peninsula, and Its Extension and Influence Abroad*. London: Cambridge University Press, 1920.

An extended form of a course of lectures given by Thomas at Cambridge in 1917, designed "to provide a comprehensive view of a literary movement which began about the turn of the fifteenth century, flourished, and died completely." The chivalric romance in France is dealt with, pp. 199–221; in England, pp. 242–301. A short bibliography is arranged according to the titles of the various Spanish romances, and an appendix, "Anthony Munday and Lazarus Pyott," presents Thomas' opinion of a puzzling question of translations. Well-indexed as to subjects, titles of literary works, and persons. Reviewed in *MP*, 1923, by G. T. Northup, who finds the most original and valuable part the chapter on the influence of the romances on Elizabethan drama. Also found in Spanish, translated by Esteban Pujals (see entry 121).

[143] ———. "The English Translations of Guevara's Works," in *Estudios eruditos in Memoriam de Adolfo Bonilla y San Martín*, Vol. II. Madrid: Imprenta Viuda e Hijos de Jaime Ratés, 1930.

Thomas states that Guevara was the first Spanish author to be translated into English prose, the most popular Spanish author in England during his own century, and that his works influenced many English writers. Thomas examines the English translations of Guevara which are now in the British Museum and deals with them as they appeared in English chronologically. He considers recent scholarship on this subject, disapproving of some. In weighing the reasons for Guevara's popularity in England, Thomas reminds the reader that this Spanish writer was even more widely acclaimed on the Continent.

[144] Thompson, Elbert N. S. *Literary Bypaths of the Renaissance.* New Haven: Yale University Press, 1924.

Thompson's inquiry into the lesser genres of the Renaissance includes character books, courtesy books, and personal letters. Although the references to Spanish writers are infrequent, some information concerning such authors as Vives, Guevara, and Gracián will be found, since the author finds them instrumental in the evolution of the genres he considers. Such information will be found in the index under the author's name or under his works.

[145] Ticknor, George. *History of Spanish Literature.* 3 vols. Boston: Houghton, Osgood, and Company, 1879.

This classic work remains a valuable source book for comparative literature researchers. Ticknor provides an excellent index (III, 533–632), which includes abundant references to English and French writers who borrowed from or were inspired by Spanish authors. The student should consult the index under the name of the author he is studying.

[146] Tucker, Thomas G. *The Foreign Debt of English Literature.* London: George Bell & Sons, 1907.

Tucker concludes his inquiry into Spanish-English literary relations (pp. 217–230) by characterizing the Spanish literature of the seventeenth century as "barren" and without much effect on England. "It is a literature wordy in expression, lacking in insight, and seldom concerning itself with the deeper interests of human life," he remarks. A synoptical table (p. 230) forms a "brief conspectus of Spanish literature" which notes some Spanish influences on English literature, in spite of the author's statement quoted above. This work is interesting, if only for the contrast it furnishes to criticism more appreciative of the Spanish contribution.

[147] Turgenev, Ivan. "Hamlet and Don Quixote," in *The Anatomy of "Don Quijote,"* M. J. Benardete and Angel Flores, editors. Ithaca, New York: The Dragon Press, 1932.

Turgenev presents a psychological interpretation of these two characters, with the theme that they represent an antithesis in personality types: Hamlet is the prototype of the egoist, while Don Quijote is the prototype of the altruist. Commenting upon this, Lester G. Crocker, in "*Hamlet, Don Quijote, La Vida es sueño,* the Quest for Values" (q.v.), finds this analysis "not particularly fruitful."

[148] Underhill, John Garrett. *Spanish Literature in the England of the Tudors.* ("Columbia University Studies in Literature.") New York: The Macmillan Company, 1899.

Careful, objective survey of the whole field of Spanish-English literary relations to date. Underhill traces these relations from the political events of the twelfth century until the close of the sixteenth century. He notes that the Elizabethan drama took from Mexía and Montemayor, the Jacobean from Cervantes and his contemporaries. Excellent historical background material is interwoven throughout. Three bibliographies are included: (1) Spanish works published in the original or in translation in Tudor England; (2) occasional literature relating to Spain, printed in Tudor England; (3) books consulted by the author on the contact of Spain and England before the death of Elizabeth.

[149]   Ungerer, Gustav. *Anglo-Spanish Relations in Tudor Literature.*
("Schweizer Anglistische Arbeiten—Swiss Studies in English.") Bern: Francke, 1956.

Ungerer divides his work into three parts: Part I deals with the effect of *La Celestina*, which he finds influential on the behavior of Elizabethan courtiers; Part II makes a study of the Elizabethan courtier; Part III is devoted to Shakespeare's drama. This last is marred by Ungerer's reliance on conjectures or inferences to establish Spanish influence on Shakespeare, calling Armado in *Love's Labour's Lost* a burlesque on the Spanish courtier Antonio Pérez. Ungerer's work contains a bibliography and seven appendices, No. 7 of which is a comparison of Sir Philip Sidney and Juan Vásquez. Reviewed in *HR*, 1957, by Edwin B. Knowles, who calls it "a valuable addition to an as yet uncrowded shelf" but notes also that it "promises too much."

[150]   Valle Abad, Federico del. *Influencia española sobre la literatura francesa: Juan Rotrou (1609–1650).* Avila: Senén Martín, 1946.

The author considers the dramatist Rotrou in relation to the *novela de caballería*, the *novela pastoril*, and in relation to Lope de Vega and Cervantes. This study includes a useful table which contains the names of authors who lived during the period under consideration, with a list of characters in their plays. A short bibliography and bibliographical textual notes are provided.

[151]   Van Roosbroeck, Gustave L. *The Cid Theme in France in 1600.* Minneapolis: Pioneer Printers, 1920.

Van Roosbroeck turns his attention to a novel by Du Périer, *La Hayne et l'amour d'Arnoul et de Clairemonde* (1600), as he searches for indications of the presence of the Spanish Cid theme. He concludes that a prior source for both Du Périer and Guillén de Castro existed in Spain before Castro wrote *Las Mocedades del Cid.*

[152]   Van Tieghem, Philippe. *Les Influences étrangères sur la littérature française, 1550–1880.* Paris: Presses Universitaires de France, 1961.

Chapter II, pp. 36–59—"Les Influences espagnoles (1600–1720)." Van Tieghem presents his conclusions concerning these influences in separate parts which concentrate on the novel, poetry, the drama, and Cervantes. He sees the Spanish influence strong at the end of the Renaissance and during the neo-classic period, but weak from 1720 to 1820. The Spanish mystics, he believes, exerted the least influence because the strong French religious tradition resisted the tendency toward mysticism. Bibliographical notes are included, as is a useful list of the translations of the principal foreign works influential on French literature from 1495 onward.

[153] Vermeylen, Alphonse. *Sainte Thérèse en France au XVIIᵉ siècle, 1600–1660.* ("Receuil de travaux d'histoire et de philologie," 4ᵉ série.) Louvain: Univérsité de Louvain, 1958.

A general survey of Teresian mysticism in France, 1600–1660, and of the influence it exercised upon Camus, Cyprien de la Nativité, Richeome, Sermond, Surin, Richelieu, Desmarets de Saint-Sorlin, Bérulle, and on Port-Royal. Robert Ricard, reviewing this study in *BH*, 1960, comments that the author is "too timid," and that he gives the impression of hardly believing his own theory.

[154] Villey-Desmeserets, Pierre. *Les Sources d'idées au seizième siècle: textes choisis et commentés.* Paris: Librairie Plon, 1912.

Of great interest to comparatists will be Chapter V, "Traductions de prosateurs espagnols," pp. 199–254. Here the author shows that Spanish ideas became important in France and other countries through the medium of French translations. In his consideration of these translations Villey-Desmeserets examines books in three categories and studies the achievement of translators in each, as follows: (1) "Le roman"—Herberay des Essarts, translator of *Amadís de Gaula*; (2) "La philosophie morale"—Guterry, translator of Guevara; Gruget, translator of Pedro Mexía; (3) "Les histoires de pays lointains"—Simon Goulard and Martin Fumée, translators of accounts of the New World. The works of Francisco López de Gómara, who wrote of his experiences with Cortés in America (as in his *Historia general de las Indias*), are seen to be Montaigne's chief source of knowledge about the Indies. Villey-Desmeserets comments, however, that since Gómara is "un écrivain très fantaisiste, j'imagine qu'il a souvent induit Montaigne en erreur."

This book is fascinating reading, but unfortunately it is not indexed, and it contains neither footnotes nor bibliography.

[155]   Vossler, Karl. *Algunos caracteres de la cultura española.* Buenos Aires: Espasa-Calpe, 1942. (Appeared first in *Deutsche Vierteljahrschrift für Literaturwissenschaft und Geistesgeschichte,* Vol. VIII, 1930.)

A cultural analysis which seeks to trace the diffusion of ideas which are found in Spanish literature and shows the intellectual currents of the Golden Age widening out to be felt in all parts of Europe in the section on "Trascendencia europea de la cultura española," pp. 87–150. Bibliographical notes are included.

[156]   Wade, Gerald E. "The Character of Don Juan of *El Burlador de Sevilla,*" pp. 167–178 in *Hispanic Studies in Honor of Nicholson B. Adams,* edited by John E. Keller and Karl-Ludwig Selig. Chapel Hill, N.C.: University of North Carolina Press, 1966.

Although not a comparative study in itself, this essay will be of interest to the researcher in comparative criticism and methodology, for as he says, Wade bases his searching analysis of Don Juan's charcter partly on a procedure explicated by Morris Weitz in his *Hamlet and the Philosophy of Literary Criticism* (Chicago, 1964), commending Weitz's effort to "order the philosophy of criticism so that scholars may criticize on a more meaningful basis." This work is Wade's contribution to the formulation of a universal method, based upon description rather than explanation and evaluation, which may be pertinent to the analysis of human character in any given work of literature. Wade emphasizes the handicap the twentieth-century student faces when he attempts to gain cultural empathy with the seventeenth century, pointing out the difficulty of understanding the workings of the Renaissance mind, whether it be represented by a Hamlet or a Don Juan.

[157] Ward, Arthur W. *The History of English Dramatic Literature to the Death of Queen Anne.* 3 vols. London: Macmillan Co., Ltd. New York: The Macmillan Company, 1899.

A thorough, detailed, well-documented history of literature which gives plentiful references to Spanish sources and influences. It will be necessary to look for these under subject, title, or author in the index. The index, which is found at the back of Vol. III, is adequate.

[158] Watson, Foster, editor. *Vives and the Renascence Education of Women.* New York: Longmans, Green & Co., 1912.

In writing his introduction to this collection of Juan Vives' works, Watson emphasizes the role played by Vives and his patroness, Catharine of Aragon, Henry VIII's queen. Vives, befriended by Thomas More and other humanists, lived in England, where he wrote works on pedagogy which were much admired and emulated by cultured English men and women. Watson comments, "Vives summarizes the best social and religious outlook, not only of his contemporaries, but even of his successors, for the whole Tudor period."

[159] Wharey, James Blanton. *Bunyan's "Mr. Badman" and the Picaresque Novel.* ("Texas University Studies in English," No. 4.) Austin: University of Texas Press, 1924.

Wharey traces the history of the picaresque novel from its beginnings with the Spanish *Lazarillo* and *Guzmán* through the English versions of this genre up through John Bunyan's *Life and Death of Mr. Badman* (1680), showing how the increasing degeneration of moral standards represented in the English picaresque culminates in Richard Head and Francis Kirkman's *The English Rogue*, published in three parts from 1666 to 1680. Wharey notes the great popularity of *The English Rogue* and characterizes it as being "full of salacious, brutal or simply nasty incidents." Bunyan's purpose, he remarks, was to pillory the evils of the age with the intent to make them repulsive by their realistic presentation. Thus *Mr. Badman* can be called a picaresque novel, Wharey concludes, since it does have an anti-hero who transgresses many rules of conduct but never outsteps the bounds of civil law; on the other hand, it does lack some of the elements of this Spanish genre because it does not purport to be autobiographical, nor does it create in the mind of the reader sympathy for the "hero," as such works as *Lazarillo* do.

Articles

[160]   Allen, Don Cameron. "Jacques' 'seven ages' and Pedro Mexía,"
        MLN, LVI (1941), 601–603.
        Commenting upon certain suggestions put forth concern-
        ing possible sources of Shakespeare's "seven ages" pas-
        sage in *As You Like It*, Allen presents the theory that it
        came from Pedro Mexía's *Silva de varia lección* (1542),
        translated as *Les diverses leçons de Pierre Messis* in 1552
        by the Frenchman Claude Gruget. Allen points out that
        Chapter XL of Mexía's *lectio* includes the "seven ages" con-
        cept, presenting the French text, since it is most likely that
        this was better known to English readers in the sixteenth
        century. In response to the question of whether or not
        Shakespeare knew Mexía's book directly, Allen answers
        that it is more likely that he knew Thomas Milles' *Treasurie
        of Auncient and Modern Times*, published in 1613 but cir-
        culated in manuscript form many years before that date.

[161]   Anonymous. Letters to the Editor, *NQ*, 1874, p. 97 and p. 133.
        Two items which consider the formerly held opinion that
        Cervantes and Shakespeare died on the same day and which
        try to determine whether Spain and England were using
        "Old Style" or "New Style" time-reckoning during this
        period. (See also Corney [entry 189] and M'Carthy [entry
        270] on this subject.)

[162]   ————. "Notes on Sales: Shelton's *Don Quixote*," *LTLS*, June
        22, 1922, p. 416; August 17, 1922, p. 536.
        These two articles are of value to those who seek to trace
        the history of various editions of *Don Quijote* and some
        other works of Cervantes as they appeared in English trans-

lation. The writer gives information on the increase in monetary value of these editions over the years.

[163]   Ares Montes, José. "Una tesis francesa sobre Tirso de Molina prosista," *Insula*, XVIII (October 1963), 10.

The author brings attention to the neglected prose of Tirso de Molina, citing especially *La Historia general de la Orden de Nuestra Señora de las Mercedes, Los Cigarrales de Toledo,* and *Deleytar aprovechando.* He mentions with approval the thesis of André Nougué, the French *hispanisant, L'Oeuvre en prose de Tirso de Molina* (Toulouse, 1962), which considers the above-mentioned Tirsian works. Ares includes a detailed analysis of Nougué's work.

[164]   Atkinson, Dorothy F. "Busirane's Castle and Artidon's Cave," *MLQ*, I (1940), 185–192.

Miss Atkinson finds the long Spanish romance *Espejo de Caballerías* a possible source for three episodes in Spenser's *Faerie Queene,* Book III, cantos xi and xii, stating that Spenser probably drew upon the first (1578) and second (1585) parts of the *Mirrour,* translated by Thomas East. The text of this article and the footnotes contain minute evidence to support this. This study, which the author hopes will stimulate further research, will be of great interest to students of Spenser.

[165]   Baldensperger, Fernand. "L'arrière plan espagnol des *Maximes* de La Rochefoucauld," *RLC*, XVI (1936), 45–62.

Baldensperger calls the combination of the Spanish *agudeza* with the "clairvoyante psychologie générale" of the seventeenth-century salons, especially that of Mme de Sablé, "une de ces alchimies comme on en trouve fréquemment dans l'histoire littéraire." No specific Spanish proverbs, however, are given to compare with the French ones which the author quotes.

[166]   Barine, Arvède. "Les Gueux d'Espagne: *Lazarillo de Tormes,*" *RDM*, LXXXVI (15 avril 1888), 870–904.

This excellent essay takes Lazarillo as a guide through the "société équivoque" of Spain during the sixteenth century, compares Lazarillo with his counterparts in France under Francis I and Henry II and like types in other countries. Barine presents the theme of hunger as paramount in the tales of these men and shows how the ideal of "honor" as illustrated by Corneille's *Le Cid* was typified by the *escudero* in *Lazarillo*.

[167] Barrès, Maurice. "Les liens spirituels de la France et de l'Espagne," *RDM*, XXI (15 juin 1924), 913–918.

In form this is a plan of a speech which Barrès had planned to deliver to the *Chambre* in favor of teaching Spanish in the schools of France. He points out the need for the French people to become aware of their debts to Spanish literature, some of which he enumerates here.

[168] Barton, Frances B. "The Sources of the Story of *Sesostris et Timarète* in *Le Grand Cyrus*," *MP*, XIX (1921–22), 257–268.

An attempt to solve the problem of sources for Mlle de Scudéry's story in the sixth volume of *Le Grand Cyrus*. Miss Barton believes that the principal source is *Los Prados de León*, a comedy by Lope de Vega. Pointing out that "in every essential episode the story of *Sesostris et Timarète* follows with absolute fidelity the action of the Spanish play," she goes on to analyze the plots of both works. In conclusion Miss Barton notes how skillfully Mlle de Scudéry has blended the predominant Spanish theme with details taken from other sources.

[169] Beberfall, Lester. "The *Pícaro* in Context," *Hispania*, XXXVII (1954), 288-292.

Beberfall presents a re-examination of Roberto Payró's *El Casamiento de Laucha*, *Lazarillo de Tormes*, Defoe's *Moll Flanders*, and Mateo Alemán's *Guzmán de Alfarache* to contest the popular idea that the *pícaro* is a conscienceless rogue. The author sees the creator of picaresque novels as "satisfying the self-appointed watch-dogs of society," at least in externals.

[170] Benardete, M. J. "Góngora Revaluated," *REH*, I (1928), 365–389.

An essay written to commemorate the four-hundredth anniversary of Góngora's death, in which Benardete expresses the opinion that recent scholarship has revealed the universal significance of the Spanish writer's work. Although seventeenth-century England saw some translations of his lyric poetry, in general Góngora has been misunderstood, if noticed at all, in later centuries because of his style, which often seems obscure. Hispanists are hoping that a revaluation of Góngora will lead to renewed interest in his writings.

[171]   Birkhead, Henry. "The Schism of England: Calderón's Play and Shakespeare's," *ML*, X (1928), 36–44.

A comparison of the treatments given by Calderón and Shakespeare to the historical events surrounding England's breaking away from the Catholic Church. Birkhead points out that the endings of the plays demonstrate the attitudes of Spain and England toward this schism: Calderón's *La Cisma* ends on a note of vengeance, while *Henry VIII* closes with a promise of happier times. Calderón changes history by having Henry revert to the Church; Shakespeare's play relies to a greater degree on fact, Birkhead states, but he adds, too, that Shakespeare's happy ending was achieved by the playwright's choosing to end the play before the other dire events had occurred.

[172]   Bohning, William H. "Lope's *El Mayor impossible* (1615) and Boisrobert's *La folle gageure* (1653)," *HR*, XII (1944), 248–257.

A carefully tabulated comparison of these two plays from which the author concludes that "the French comedy is a very free translation, scene by scene, of the Spanish play and that Boisrobert's *Advis au lecteur* exaggerates the importance of the changes introduced and slights his accomplishment as a free translator."

[173]   Bond, R. Warwick. "On Six Plays in *Beaumont and Fletcher, 1679*," *RES*, XI (1935), 257–275.

Bond finds that the main action of *Love's Cure* is closely borrowed from a comedy by the poet Guillén de Castro, *Le*

Fuerza de la costumbre, although in the English play the material is enlarged and improved. Bond gives his version of the Spanish piece with the insertion of references to the English play; he indicates his disagreement with the remark in the *Cambridge History of English Literature* (VI, 140) which admits no ground for the supposition that the two plays are comparable.

[174] Brandès, George. "Don Quixote and Hamlet," *FoR*, C (October 1913), 652–660.

An imaginary and amusing encounter between Don Quixote and Hamlet in which the two heroes pledge brotherhood and ride off to build the "Church of the Future." The conversations between the two "knights" embody interpretations of their possible significance as representations of human ideals.

[175] Brault, Gerard J. "English Translations of the *Celestina* in the Sixteenth Century," *HR*, XXVIII (1960), 301–312.

Brault presents a scholarly survey of the editions of Rojas' work in sixteenth-century England. He notes that Anthony Munday's allusion to the *Celestina* in his *Second and Third Blast of Retrait from Plaies and Theaters* (1580) is a "valuable indication that the *Celestina* was probably popular among English people who could read it in Spanish or in a Continental translation," for there is evidence of only one translation (1598) between Rastell's in 1530 and Mabbe's in 1630 to provide the English public with Rojas' work in the English language.

[176] Brunetière, Ferdinand. "Corneille et le théâtre espagnol," *RDM*, XIII (1903), 189–216.

A noteworthy article on comparative literature in general, incident to the author's *critique* of *P. Corneille et le théâtre espagnol* by Huszár, *La Comédia espagnole en France de Hardy à Racine*, by Martinenche, and *Corneille* by Gustave Lanson. The article includes a summary of the history of Spanish-French literary relations. (The three books mentioned above may be found in our section on books.)

[177] ———. "L'Influence de l'Espagne dans la littérature française," *RDM*, CIV (mai 1891), 215–226.

This essay was occasioned by the appearance of Morel-Fatio's first *Études sur l'Espagne* (see entry 107), which work Brunetière welcomes as a meritorious addition to the meager amount of knowledge available to the literary historian concerning a literature which "a . . . agi . . . plus profondément et plus continûment" than any other on the French literature. Thorough as ever, Brunetière presents a brief sketch of the fortunes of Spanish works in France from the period of the courtly romances to his own times.

[178] Buceta, Erasmo. "Voltaire y Cervantes," *RFE*, VII (1920), 60–61.

A note on the prejudiced treatment given to Spanish literature by Voltaire. Buceta points out, however, that Voltaire in 1756 declared that Spanish literature was a model for other literatures. It was in 1771 that Voltaire reversed himself, saying that there was nothing valuable in the literature of Spain but *Don Quijote*. Voltaire's first remark was made in his *Essai sur les moeurs et l'esprit des nations*, the second in a letter to M. Tabareau.

[179] Buchanan, Milton A. "A Neglected Version of Quevedo's 'Romance' on Orpheus," *MLN*, XX (1905), 116–118.

Buchanan considers Quevedo's verse "romance" (translated into English by Lady Monck in 1716) about Orpheus' trip to the lower regions to find a wife, locating the original in "Flor de los mejores romances," which was published as early as 1623, and republished in Quevedo's *Obras completas* in Sevilla in 1903.

[180] Büchner, A. "Comparaison des théâtres de l'Espagne et de l'Angleterre," *RB*, VII (25 juin 1870), 490–496.

This is a concise and informative summing up of the comparative characteristics of Spanish, French, and English drama from the sixteenth century through the seventeenth century. The author provides a comparison also of Shakespeare and Calderón in their treatment of the themes of jealousy and heresy.

[181]   Cadorel, Raymond. "Les Nouvelles espagnoles du *Roman comique*," *RLC*, XXXVI (1962), 244–252.

A consideration of the four *novelle* "au sein même du *Roman comique*," used by Scarron. Cadorel uses as his point of departure the judgments of George Hainsworth in this analysis of Scarron's debt to Solórzano, noting as he does so the varying attitudes of critics toward these *novelle*.

[182]   Carayon, Marcel. "L'Amour et la musique; sur un passage de *La Celestina*," *RLC*, III (1923), 419–421.

An intriguing discussion of the similar treatment of love and music in *La Celestina* and *Twelfth Night* by Shakespeare. Carayon sees the passage of *Twelfth Night* in which the Duke says, "If music be the food of love, play on," as an echo of the beginning of *La Celestina* where Calisto tells Sempronio, "Pero tañe et canta la más triste canción que sepas," and considers both of these passages as illustrations of the general theme of "vague des passions." He admits that we cannot know if Shakespeare was acquainted with Rojas' play and that we base our guesses on the existence of an Italian translation of the Spanish work or on the likelihood that Shakespeare knew the MS. of Mabbe (circulated in 1631) through Ben Jonson, a friend of Mabbe.

[183]   Cazenave, Jean. "Le roman hispano-mauresque en France," *RLC*, V (1925), 594–640.

A tracing of the evolution of the type of French novel which deals with romantic subjects and which has as heroes Moors in Spain. Finding the origin of this theme in the works of Ginés Pérez de Hita, Cazenave notes that "Pérez de Hita et ses imitateurs français sont responsables de la conception erronée que nous avons de cette civilisation lointaine," and makes the point that the novels presented as models of courage, gallantry, and virtue men who were actually rude, unpolished Spaniards or decadent, scheming Moors.

[184]   Chapman, K. P. "*Lazarillo de Tormes*, a Jest-Book, and Benedick," *MLR*, LV (1960), 565–567.

Chapman thinks that Benedick's comment, "Ho, now you

strike like the blindman, twas the boy that stole your meate, and youle beate the post," in Shakespeare's *Much Ado About Nothing* (II, i, 206–207) refers to *Lazarillo de Tormes*, since this Spanish picaresque novel formed the basis of a popular jestbook in Shakespeare's time. Chapman, however, does not attribute a direct knowledge of Spanish literature to Shakespeare.

[185] Clément, Louis. "Antoine de Guevara, ses lecteurs et ses imitateurs français au XVIe siècle," *RHLF*, VII (1900), 590–602; VIII (1901), 214–233.

Noting that Guevara "eut peut-être à l'étranger plus lecteurs que dans sa patrie," Clément presents a scholarly two-part study of Guevara's importance in European affairs. Part I—"Les traités sur *La Cour* de Guevara et le *Courtisan retiré* de Jean de la Taille." In the seventeenth century Hardy used the *Aviso de privados y doctrina de Cortesanos* as the basis for his *Reveille-matin des courtisans.* Part II—"Les épistres dorées de Guevara comparées aux *Diverses leçons* de Pierre Messie à la suite d'Antoine du Verdier, au *Recueil d'aucuns cas merveilleux* de Jean de Marcouville, et aux *Essais* de Montaigne." Detailed, interesting study of "la moral anecdotique" and the influence of Guevara's work. Of especial interest to students of the seventeenth century is "Ce que Montaigne doit aux continuateurs de Guevara," pp. 224–233.

[186] Collmer, Robert G. "Crashaw's 'Death More Misticall and High,'" *JEGP*, LV (1956), 373–380.

Crashaw's poem, written as the subtitle indicates, "In memory of the Vertuous and Learned Lady Madre de Teresa that sought an early Martyrdome," was published in his *Steps to the Temple* in 1646. Collmer states that he follows Austin Warren's lead in tracing Catholic mystic thought within Crashaw's poetry as he interprets the poet as referring to the death of the soul, not of the body. Weighing the various Renaissance meanings for the word "death," he decides that they are inadequate to define death as it is found in the context of Crashaw's poems, and goes on to elaborate on his assertion that this "death" must refer to a spiritual phenomenon.

[187]   Cordasco, Francesco. "Smollett and the Translation of the *Don Quijote*," *MLQ*, XIII (1952), 23–36.

A scholarly note which praises the translation of *Don Quijote* which appeared in England in 1755 through the efforts of Isaiah Pettigrew as translator and Tobias Smollett as reviser and consultant. Cordasco also quotes expressions of approval of David Hannay and Francisco Rodríguez Marín.

[188]   ———. "Spanish Influence on Restoration Drama: George Digby's *Elvira* (1663)," *RLC*, XXVII (1953), 93–98.

A study of the parallels of early Restoration comedy with some plays of Lope de Vega, Calderón, and Tirso de Molina, in which Cordasco points out the similarities in methods, plots, and motivations and suggests that "the English comedy of intrigue from 1660–1670 owes its vitality to the Spanish drama instead of the French," seeing *Elvira* as being heavily influenced by Calderón's *No siempre lo peor es cierto*. (Digby was a translator of Calderón.) Cordasco quotes parallel passages from Calderón's play and *Elvira*.

[189]   Corney, Bolton. "Shakespeare and Cervantes," *Athenaeum*, XXVI, Pt. 1 (April 1864), 475.

This letter to the editor discussses the dates of the deaths of Shakespeare and Cervantes, calling a fiction the "current assumption" that they died on the same day.

[190]   Coster, Adolphe. "Baltasar Gracián," *RH*, XXIX (décembre 1913), 347–754.

A lengthy study of Gracián which presents a biography, analyses of his works, and a consideration of his influence. "Gracián hors d'Espagne," pp. 666–688, tells of his fame in France and England, which Coster declares was even greater than it was in Spain. This section considers the evidence for Gracián's influence on La Rochefoucauld, Saint-Évremond, Fénelon, and Vauvenargues.

[191] ———. "Corneille a-t-il connu *El Héroe* de Baltasar Gracián?" *RH*, XLVI (juin–aôut 1919), 569–672.

Coster believes that a passage from *Horace* (1640) by Corneille was derived directly from Gracián's *El Héroe* (1639), this passage in *Horace* being in Act V, sc. ii, vss. 1555–1580, in spite of certain scholars' objections that Corneille had not known the Spanish book at that time. Pertinent lines from Corneille and Gracián are provided as illustration.

[192] Crawford, J. P. Wickersham. "A Sixteenth Century Spanish Analogue of *Measure for Measure*," *MLN*, XXXV (1920), 330–334.

Characterizing the play *Comedia del Degollado* by Juan de la Cueva as "one of the best composed in Spain . . . before the appearance of Lope de Vega," Crawford points out some of its parallels with Shakespeare's play, although his emphasis is on the general theme of the two plays, not on detailed analysis.

[193] Crocker, L. G. "*Hamlet, Don Quijote, La Vida es sueño*: the Quest for Values," *PMLA*, LXIX, Pt. 1 (1954), 278–313.

A thought-provoking study based on the author's belief that each of the heroes in these works is involved in situations where the problem of evil in men becomes the key to his conduct as he searches for a way out of moral anarchy. The existentialist overtones in these three works are carefully considered.

[194] Dabney, Lancaster C. "A Sixteenth Century French Account of the Spanish Armada," *MLN*, LVI (1946), 265–267.

This short article concerns a play by Antoine Lancel which appeared in 1604 and which Dabney calls "violent, partisan, Protestant propaganda," which is somewhat redeemed by Lancel's sincerity and real patriotism. The play, though not of much literary value, provides historical interest because of its revelation of some seventeenth-century attitudes toward the fate of the Armada, a recurrent theme in contemporary European literature.

[195] Dale, G. I. "La Rochefoucauld and Cervantes," *MLN*, XLVI (1931), 519–520.

In response to some scholarship which has sought to demonstrate that the *maxime* of La Rochefoucauld, "Le soleil ni la mort ne se peuvent regarder fixement," was taken from Cervantes' *El Licenciado vidriera*, Dale declares that there is no real evidence to support the contention that the French writer took this *maxime* from the above *novela* or any other work of Cervantes.

[196] Darmangeat, Pierre. "Cervantès et nous," *Europe*, LXXVI (avril 1952), 97–102.

Darmangeat presents Cervantes as a Christian, but not as an orthodox Catholic; he interprets the Spanish writer as a man of reason who has a universal appeal, one which becomes more valid as we move toward a new "Age of Gold" predicated on the ideals of true Christianity.

[197] Davril, R. E. "John Ford and La Cerda's *Inés de Castro*," *MLN*, LXVI (1951), 464–466.

Writing of the amazing final scene of Ford's *The Broken Heart* Davril finds parallels in the Spanish legend of Bernardo del Carpio and the legend of Inés de Castro in the Spanish version. This latter legend was one of the most popular in Portugal and Spain, and *The Broken Heart* was written at a time when Beaumont and Fletcher were using Spanish subjects. This article, however, does not prove direct borrowing from a Spanish play but merely notes the use of a "post-mortem coronation and wedding from Spanish tradition."

[198] Doumic, R. "Le drame espagnol et notre théâtre classique," *RDM*, I (15 février 1901), 920–931.

A consideration of the essential nature of the *comedia*, which Doumic says is to be credited with providing the guide by which the French theater found its way to greatness, for Spanish models furnished "les véritables ressorts dramatiques," love and the concept of honor. He comments upon Corneille, noting his relation to the *comedia* and to the neo-classical rules.

[199]   Dreano, M. "Monsieur de Queriolet and Dom Juan," *RHLF*,
        LXII (1962), 503–513.
        Dreano ponders the question of the origin of Molière's
        character of Don Juan and comes to the conclusion that
        Molière had a mind original enough to create without bor-
        rowing, although, since in 1660 "les Dom Juans couraient
        les rues," the French playwright might have been influenced
        by Tirso de Molina's *El Burlador de Sevilla* or the Italian
        versions of this play. From a more minute examination of
        the evidence Dreano favors the Italian influence, seeing
        more resemblances in Molière's play to the Italian story of
        Queriolet, which appeared in France in 1630; in addition,
        Dreano points out that "La scène du pauvre [who begged
        alms of Don Juan] n'existe pas dans le *Burlador*," and be-
        lieves it quite possible that Molière had never read Tirso's
        play.

[200]   Entwistle, William J. "Benedick and Lazarillo," *LTLS*, Sep-
        tember 30, 1926, p. 654.
        Entwistle states his disapproval of those who would find
        in *Lazarillo* the source for the passage in Shakespeare's
        Much Ado about Nothing (II, i) which begins, "Ho, now
        you strike like a blind man." He declares that this case is
        much more complicated, averring that the incident of the
        stone pillar is related in Sebastián de Horozco's *Cancionero*
        six years before *Lazarillo* was published, and suggesting that
        it may be possible that Horozco is the unknown author of
        this first picaresque novel. Entwistle, however, scores the
        "trivialities of 'source-hunting.' "

[201]   ———. "Honra y duelo," *RJ*, III (1950), 404–420.
        Saying that the concepts of *honra*, *respeto*, *fama*, and
        opinión found in the Golden Age Spanish drama have been
        interpreted many times, Entwistle points out that the word
        duelo has been neglected. During the course of his analysis
        of this concept he notes a parallel between Calderón's *Las
        Armas de la hermosura* and Shakespeare's *Coriolanus*, spe-
        cifically in regard to the honorable citizen's duty to the state.

[202]   Esler, Anthony. "Robert Greene and the Spanish Armada,"
        ELH, XXXII (1965), 314–332.

Esler's concern is Greene's single venture into the realm of war propaganda with his *Spanish Masquerado* (1589), a satirical assault on Spain prompted by the English defeat of the Armada in 1588. This play disappeared from sight as the battle became remote, but it represents, as Esler remarks, the mood of the English people in a moment of triumph over a hated enemy and constitutes an example of "journalistic jubilation" on Greene's part. Esler sees in this play also symbols of Elizabethan attitudes toward Catholicism and of collective fear of the international power of Spain.

[203]   Eyer, Cortland. "Boisrobert's *La vraye Didon ou La Didon chaste*," RR, XXXII (1941), 329–338.

From his examination of the evidence concerning Boisrobert's Spanish sources, Eyer concludes that it is likely that Boisrobert was indebted for the conception of his Dido to either or both of the two Spanish dramas, Lasso de la Vega's *Honra de Dido restaurada* and Virués' *Elisa Dido*. Before this time Justin had been assumed to be the main source of Boisrobert's play. Eyer presents his evidence in the form of quotations from the Spanish writers and from Boisrobert.

[204]   Fabié, Antonio María. "Cómo nos juzgan los franceses," ReE, XCVI (enero-febrero 1884), 19–31.

The purpose of this article is to prove the superiority of the Spanish drama to the "imitaciones franceses" of Corneille, Molière, and others. Fabié takes especial note of the French debt to Ruiz de Alarcón's *La Verdad sospechosa*, often cited as Corneille's source for *Le Menteur*. Fabié's essay may be found also in Barry's edition of Alarcón's play under the title, "Vindicación apologética de *La Verdad sospechosa*." (Of this edition Warren T. McCready comments in his *Bibliografía temática de Estudios sobre el Teatro Español Antiguo*, "Barry equivocó . . . el año.")

[205]   Fellheimer, Jeannette. "Hellowes' and Fenton's Translations of Guevara's *Epístolas Familiares*," SP, XLIV (1947), 140–156.

With the statement that "the vogue of Antonio Guevara

in sixteenth-century England was instantaneous and profound," Miss Fellheimer surveys the extent of his influence via the translations into English, coming to the conclusion that his notable influence was reflected in the "general impetus rather than definite models" which he gave to letter-writers. She credits Guevara with stimulating an interest in the epistles of Seneca, thus directing English writers toward a style typified by the Baconian essay. The article includes parallel passages from Guevara and some English translations of his work.

[206]   Fischer, Walther. "Honoré d'Urfé's *Sireine* and the *Diana* of Montemayor," *MLN*, XXVIII (1913), 166–169.

Fischer notes that *Sireine* was composed some time before *L'Astrée* and shows that some parts of the former are direct translations of the Spanish *Diana*; many other parts freely enlarge upon Montemayor's work. Fischer finds d'Urfé's text independent of Nicolas Colin's translation of *Diana* (1572) and provides quotations from the *Sireine* to show how Montemayor's "niceties, concetti, and plays on words" are preserved.

[207]   Fitzmaurice-Kelly, James. "Cervantes and Shakespeare," *PBA*, VII (1916), 297–317.

This article adds to the literature of speculation on the subject of Cervantes' knowledge of Shakespeare and Shakespeare's knowledge of Cervantes. Fitzmaurice-Kelly admits that it is more likely that Cervantes influenced the great Englishman than the reverse, suggesting that it is not impossible that Shakespeare had read some of the Spaniard's writings and finding parallels and contrasts in the two writers' works.

[208]   ———. "Cervantes in England," *PBA*, II (1905–1906), 11–29. (Read January 25, 1905, in commemoration of the tercentenary of *Don Quijote*.)

The author asserts that the ground was prepared for Cervantes in England by previous translations of Spanish works such as *Amadís de Gaula* and *Diana*, that England was the first foreign country to mention *Don Quijote*, the first to provide a critical edition of the text of this novel, and that for three centuries English writers have turned to Cervantes for inspiration. Specific mention of such writers as Shakespeare, Fletcher, Field, Shelton, Drayton, Butler, Massinger, and Davenant enhances the interest of this article.

[209]   ———. "Some Correlations of Spanish Literature," *RH*, XV (1906), 58–85.

Early Spanish influences in England which led to a later, stronger interest in Spain are traced here by the famous Hispanist. He sees the first step to "sustained intellectual commerce" between Spain and England as being taken when Caxton, the printer, included in his *Aesop* (1483) thirteen of the *Fables of Alfonse* by Pedro Alfonso. The commerce was strengthened further by knowledge in England of Luis Vives, *La Celestina*, and Guevara. Through North's translation of Guevara's *Reloj de príncipes con el Libro de Marco Aurelio* as *Diall of Princes* (1557), Fitzmaurice-Kelly sees a possible Spanish influence on Shakespeare.

[210]   Foulché-Delbosc, R. "Mme d'Aulnoy et l'Espagne," *RH*, LXVII (1926), 1–151.

This thorough and well-documented article studies the life and works of Mme d'Aulnoy, eighteenth-century *hispanisante*, who was instrumental in bringing Spanish literature to the attention of her countrymen by her books *Mémoires de la cour d'Espagne* (1690) and *Relation du voyage d'Espagne* (1691). It is doubtful that Mme d'Aulnoy ever visited Spain and, Foulché points out, her books were nothing but compilations of works of other authors; up to 1865, however, she was credited with writing first-hand accounts of her travels. Appendix C of this study contains a list of the sources used by Mme d'Aulnoy and parallel passages from her *Mémoires* and from various of her sources. Foulché does not consider the literary effects of the popularity of the Frenchwoman's delineation of Spain, but he gives valuable information and interpretation useful to the literary historian.

[211]   Fournier, Édouard. "L'Espagne et ses comédiens en France au XVIIe siècle," *RH*, XXV (1911), 19–46.

A review of the historical events which led to the vogue of things Spanish in France. Fournier notes that Anne d'Autriche, Louis XIII's queen, was instrumental in the sudden rise of interest in Spain and subsequent decline of Italian influence. With this new emphasis came the Spanish literary influence, seen notably in the works of Thomas Corneille, Boisrobert, Quinault, Scarron, and Molière, inspired by Lope de Vega, Solís, Moreto, Antonio de Mendoza, Fernando de Zárate, Tirso de Molina, and Calderón. Interesting also for its close comparisons of specific Spanish and French plays and their historical backgrounds.

[212]   Fucilla, Joseph G. "Spanish Poetry in English to the Year 1850," *Hispania*, First Special Number, January 1934, 35–44.

The author describes his work as having: (1) "A list of articles or studies containing or pointing out hitherto unrecorded or little known translations and imitations"; and (2) "A list of new translations drawn from an extensive survey of periodical and book literature." From his research Fucilla concludes that Spanish poetry, as compared to French and Italian, never attained a vogue of any considerable magnitude up to 1850 in the English-speaking world. He sees only Barnabe Googe and Philip Sidney in the sixteenth century, Drummond of Hawthornden in the Elizabethan period, and various poets (influenced by Góngora) of the baroque age, as being inspired to use Spanish poetic models.

[213]   Gallas, K. R. "Les recherches de M. G. L. Van Roosbroeck autour de Corneille," *Neophilologus*, VIII (1922–1923), 248–252.

Gallas examines a number of Van Roosbroeck's books and articles, most of which are concerned with the influence of contemporary conditions in Europe and their effect upon Corneille. One of the books examined is *The Cid Theme in France before 1660* (see entry 151), about which Gallas queries, "Faut-il toujours croire à des sources?"

[214]   Gérard, Albert S. "Baroque and the Order of Love: Structural Parallels in Corneille's *Le Cid* and Vondel's *Japtha*," *Neophilologus*, XLIX (1965), 118–131.

Gérard presents a comprehensive analysis of literary theory in the baroque era, remarking that the concept of poetic justice was central to all seventeenth-century tragedy, classical or not, and that this concept was actually applied by most playwrights in Spain and elsewhere in Europe. Gérard sees literary theory based on a demand for order at this time, embodied in an hierarchy of love, honor, and devotion to the state, for the state existed to bolster this order. The author shows how the tensions created by these often conflicting loyalties are resolved in certain dramatists in Spain and France and other countries to show their espousal of the principles of universal order. Gérard sees Corneille's drama as being closely related to the *comedia*. Among the writers included in this analysis are Lope de Vega, Tirso de Molina, Calderón, Corneille, and Jean de la Taille.

[215]   Gillet, Joseph E. "A Possible New Source for Molière's *Tartuffe*," *MLN*, XLV (1930), 152–154.

Gillet puts forward Juan de Zabaleta's *El Día de fiesta por la mañana* (Madrid, 1654) as a possible source for Molière's characterization of Tartuffe, for this little known Spanish example of "character-writing" contains the portrayal of El Hypocrita, "a religious impostor, a gifted actor, self-indulgent, concupiscent, clever, and unscrupulous," in Gillet's words. Comparative passages from Zabaleta and Molière are provided to round out this study. Although Gillet is unable to prove that Molière had read Zabaleta, he finds "no objection to assuming that he may have."

[216]   ———. "Voltaire's Original Letter to Mayans about Corneille's *Héraclius*," *MLN*, XLV (1930), 34–35.

This letter was written by Voltaire June 15, 1762, to D. Gregorio Mayans, who had probably sent Voltaire a rare, undated copy of Calderón's play *En esta vida todo es verdad y todo mentira*.

[217]   ———. Glendinning, Nigel. "La Fortuna de Góngora en el siglo XVIII," *RFE*, XLIV (1961), 323–349.

This article deals mainly with Góngora's reputation in Spain during the eighteenth century, but it also contains several comments regarding English and French opinions of the Spanish poet at this time. These comments, which may be fruitful of further research, will be found in the text itself and also in the footnotes.

[218] Grant, R. Patricia. "Cervantes' *El casamiento engañoso* and Fletcher's *Rule a Wife and Have a Wife*," HR, XII (1944), 330–338.

In order to show how closely Fletcher follows Cervantes in scene, time, characters, episode, and diction in his play, Miss Grant presents parallel passages from both works, preceded by an examination of the scholarly studies done on Fletcher's Spanish debt, especially the work of Leo Bahlsen, the German scholar. Miss Grant concludes that "the common denominator within the literary contributions of Fletcher and Cervantes is ingenious inventiveness and variety of incident."

[219] Green, Otis H. "A Critical Survey of Scholarship in the Field of Spanish Renaissance Literature, 1914–1944," SP, XLIV (1947), 229–264.

A useful survey to provide background information for the student of the Renaissance in Spain. It is written, as the author indicates, from the standpoint of the history of ideas.

[220] Grierson, Herbert. "*Don Quixote*, Some Wartime Reflections on Its Character and Influence," EAP, No. 48, 1921.

A trenchant analysis of Cervantes' novel, which includes fruitful comparisons between it and certain masterpieces of English and other literatures.

[221] Grubbs, H. A. "The Originality of La Rochefoucauld's Maxims," RHLF, XXXVI (1929), 18–59.

Grubbs asserts that although La Rochefoucauld's writings show the influence of Gracián, this influence must have come through an intermediary, since the French writer knew no Spanish. His subsequent examination brings him to the conclusion that the intermediary could have been Mme de Sablé, whose writings contain fifteen maxims taken from

Gracián. The article includes the corresponding passages from Gracián, Mme de Sablé, and La Rochefoucauld.

[222] Hainsworth, George. "Quelques notes pour la fortune de Lope de Vega en France (XVIIᵉ siècle)," *BH*, XXXIII (1931), 199–213.

Hainsworth studies the impact of Lope de Vega's drama in France, omitting any consideration of his other works. Although Lope was widely imitated by many of the leading French dramatists, Hainsworth point out the tardiness with which the influence of the *comedia* was diffused abroad, for this characteristically Spanish genre was popular in Spain for twenty years before it was known in France.

[223] ———"Notes supplémentaires sur Lope de Vega en France," *BH*, XLI (1939), 352–363.

This short article supplements Hainsworth's previous study, "Quelques notes pour la fortune de Lope de Vega en France (XVIIᵉ siècle)" (q.v.).

[224] Harmand, R. "En lisant Lope de Vega: Molière doit-il deux détails de son oeuvre?" *RLC*, X (1930), 471–477.

A presentation of excerpts from Lope de Vega's *Dorotea* and Molière's *Le Misanthrope* and *L'Avare* to support Harmand's hypothesis that Molière derived his passages from Lope. The resemblances which he points out are striking.

[225] Harrison, T. P. Jr. "A Probable Source of Beaumont and Fletcher's *Philaster*," *PMLA*, XLI (1926), 294–303.

Noting that Beaumont and Fletcher generally found inspiration for their plays in Spanish romances, especially those of Cervantes, Lope de Vega, Gonzalo de Céspedes, and Mateo Alemán, Harrison discovers striking resemblances in *Philaster* to Alonso Pérez's continuation of Montemayor's *Diana*. In support of this he offers a comparison of the two, including at the same time opinions about the sources of *Philaster* as expressed by various critics.

[226] ———. "Concerning *Two Gentlemen of Verona* and Montemayor's *Diana*," *MLN*, XLI (1926), 251–252.

After a close examination of the evidence concerning Shakespeare's use of Montemayor's story of Felix and Felismena as found in the *Diana*, Harrison concludes that Shakespeare did rely on Montemayor rather than on versions of an Italian play, *Gl'Ingannati*. He thinks it is not impossible that Shakespeare read Montemayor's novel in the original Spanish; even if he did not, there were two English translations available, one by Edward Paston and one fragment by Barnabe Googe which contained the story of Felismena.

[227]   ———. "The *Faerie Queene* and the *Diana*," PQ, IX (1930), 51–56.

The author's purpose is to present two episodes in the *Faerie Queene* which reveal a considerable resemblance to certain features of the *Diana* by Montemayor's continuator, Alonso Pérez. Harrison enumerates five parallel themes, identifying the episodes in Spenser's work as (1) that concerning Pastorella and Calidor (VI, ix ff.) and (2) that concerning Placidas and Amyas (IV, vii ff.). Harrison admits that Spenser was undoubtedly influenced by Sidney, but thinks that the fact that these two writers were close friends is evidence enough to warrant assuming that Spenser shared Sidney's great admiration for Spanish pastorals.

[228]   Hart, T. R. Jr. "Sismondi as Critic of the Spanish *Comedia*," MLN, LXXI (1956), 33–37.

Hart emphasizes the objectivity of the literary criticism of Sismondi (Jean-Charles Léonard Simonde de Sismondi) as he examines the approach Sismondi takes to literature in his *De la Littérature du midi de l'Europe*, which appeared in four volumes in 1813. As an indication of Sismondi's admiration of Spanish literature, Hart calls attention to his statement (III, 363) that Spanish literature is one "à laquelle nous devons le grand Corneille."

[229]   Haškovec, P. M. "Belleforest, Zorrilla, y Rotrou," RHLF, XVII (1910), 156–157.

Haškovec analyzes the statement made by Gustave Reynier in his book *Le Roman sentimental avant "L'Astrée"* (q.v.) that the 120th "histoire" in volume 7 of Belleforest is perhaps the source from which Rojas Zorrilla took his play, *No hay ser padre siendo rey*, and also that this is a source for Rotrou's *Venceslas*. Haškovec believes that it is more likely that Zorrilla found his inspiration in Castro's *La Justicia en la piedad*, basing his opinion on internal evidence which indicates that Zorrilla's play has more traits found in Castro than in Belleforest.

[230] Hatzfeld, Helmut. "El predominio del espíritu español en la literatura europea del siglo XVII," *RFH*, III (1941), 9–23.

Hatzfeld makes a country-by-country survey of the extent to which elements of the "barroco" appear in various literatures and concludes that during the Renaissance Spain acted as a veritable guide in the literary manifestations of the mystic experience. He identifies the height of the baroque quality with Calderonian "metaforismo." Asserting that "España llevó todo su misticismo a Francia," Hatzfeld offers passages from several authors to support his comparisons.

[231] ————. "El estilo nacional en los símiles de los místicos españoles y franceses," *NRFH*, I (1947), 43–77.

A comparison of the literary styles of the Spanish and French as they are reflected in the similes used by their mystics in their writings. Hatzfeld selects various themes, then analyzes first the Spanish treatment, then the French, and finally concludes that the Spanish are inclined to express their experiences directly, while the French tend to theorize on the mystic union. Alphonse Vermeylen in *LLR*, 1951 (q.v.), believes that this synthesis is premature, coming as it does before careful studies of individuals have been made, and that Hatzfeld has not taken careful note of "profane writers" on the subject.

[232] Hazard, Paul. "Anglais, Français, Espagnols: D'après une publication récente," *RDM*, LIV (1929), 204–218.

A consideration of Salvador de Madariaga's book *Englishmen, Frenchmen, Spaniards: an Essay in Comparative Psychology* (q.v.). Hazard's essay summarizes this work, which is characterized as "un livre bienfaisant," partially based on a simplification well known since the time of Taine's formulation of the "faculté maîtresse," which Hazard sees as having some value for bringing order so that a greater measure of understanding may be created between nations.

[233] ———. "Ce que les lettres françaises doivent à l'Espagne," *RLC*, XVI (1936), 5–22.

Hazard traces the thread of Spanish literary influence upon French letters and admits, "Je suis frappé de la fidelité, de la vitalité de cette persistance," as he points out many themes and literary sources which have emanated from Spanish literature and life to enrich French letters.

[234] Hémon, Felix. "*Don Sancho d'Aragon*: De quoi est faite une comédie heroïque de Corneille," *RB*, VI, Pt. 1 (1896), 134–137.

In considering the sources of Corneille's *Don Sancho d'Aragon* Hémon finds evidence that the French poet found models for his work in a play attributed to Lope de Vega, *El Palacio confuso*, and in a novela, *Dom Pelago ou l'Entrée des maures en Espagne* (1654) by Felix de Juvenel.

[235] Hendrix, W. S. "Quevedo, Guevara, Lesage, and *The Tatler*," *MP*, XIX (1921–1922), 177–186.

The object of this article is to point out certain parallels between the *Tatler* and the Spanish writers mentioned in the title above. Hendrix comments that no one to this time, apparently, has made a comparative study of this nature, which he undertakes by emphasizing the importance in England of translations of Quevedo's *Sueños* (tr. 1709) and Lesage's *Le Diable boiteux* (tr. 1708), the latter of which was based on Guevara's *Diablo cojuelo*, and expresses his conviction that Addison and Steele would have read whatever was popular. Hendrix concludes the article with a detailed comparison of certain excerpts from the *Tatler* papers (237, 100, 110), with corresponding passages from Guevara and Lesage to bolster his argument.

[236] Herrero, Miguel. "Nueva interpretación de la novela picaresca," *RFE*, XXIV (1937), 343–362.

Herrero's thesis in his own words is that "la Picaresca es un arte naturalista que tiene dos formas, una literaria y otra plástica o pictórica. Las circunstancias históricas de la Europa post-tridentina hicieron que en España se aliase la forma literaria ascético-concinatoria y se produjese un tipo híbrido de novela-sermón, mientras en el resto de Europa se producía la pintura de género y el grabado humorístico-satírico." Special emphasis is placed on the Spanish *pícaro*; his relation to the English and French counterparts is demonstrated.

[237] Hilton, Ronald. "Four Centuries of Cervantes: the Historical Anatomy of a Best-Selling Masterpiece," *Hispania*, XXX (1947), 310–320.

Hilton ponders the question of "immortality" in a work of literature as he follows *Don Quijote* from its successful beginnings through its triumphs in England, France, and Germany (except for a period of eclipse under the neo-classicists). He concludes his informative survey on a pessimistic note for the fate of Cervantes' novel at the hands of the materially minded young people who represent the new generation.

[238] Howarth, W. D. "Cervantes and Fletcher: A Theme with Variations," *MLR*, LVI (1961), 563–566.

This brief article deals with a theme found in Cervantes' *Persiles y Sigismunda*, the ritual of the defloration of the bride practiced in some primitive societies. Cervantes' novel, translated into English in 1619 through the French version of 1617, furnished the theme of *Custom of the Country*, a drama thought to be the work of Fletcher and Massinger. Howarth makes some remarks concerning Cervantes' ethical attitude toward this custom.

[239] Huntley, F. L. "Milton, Mendoza, and the Chinese Land-Ship," *MLN*, LXIX (1954), 404–407.

Huntley accepts a Spanish friar from Toledo, Juan González de Mendoza, as the primary source of Milton's knowledge of the Chinese land-ship mentioned in *Paradise Lost*, III, 431, 442. Mendoza's book appeared in English translation in 1588 as *The Historie of the Great and Mighty King-dome of China*, and Huntley sees Milton using this source to emphasize the quality of false pride, the Catholic Span-iard being a symbol of this in seventeenth-century Pro-testant England.

[240]   Izard, Thomas C. "The Principal Source for Marlowe's *Tam-burlaine*," *MLN*, LVIII (1943), 411–417.

Marlowe scholars generally agree, Izard states, that most of *Tamburlaine's* plot comes from Pedro Mexía's *Silva de varia lección* through its first English version, Thomas Fortescue's *The Forest*. Izard, however, doubts that Marlowe knew *The Forest* and finds the source of *Tamburlaine* in a work that has been overlooked, George Whetstone's *English Myrror* (1586), in which Mexía's plot is intercalated. Parallel quotations from *Tamburlaine* and the *English Myrror* are included here.

[241]   Jacquot, Jean. "Le théâtre du monde de Shakespeare à Cal-derón," *RLC*, XXXI (1957), 341–372.

Jacquot shows how the Shakespearian and Calderonian theme of the world as a stage and man an actor on it has been used by other writers, including Kyd, Marston, Ford, Beaumont and Fletcher, Lope de Vega, Corneille, and Rotrou. He traces this theme back to such ancient writers as Seneca, Plotinus, Chrysostom, noting the last-mentioned writer as a great influence on Calderón. Too, he points out possible affinities between *King Lear* and *La Vida es sueño*.

[242]   Jessup, Mary Helen. "Rotrou's *Dom Bernard de Cabrère* and Its Source *La Próspera Fortuna de Don Bernardo de Cabre-ra*," *MLN*, XLVII (1932), 392–396.

Miss Jessup sees practically all of Rotrou's characters and situations in this play as being derived from the play of un-known authorship (often ascribed to Lope de Vega, how-ever), *La Próspera Fortuna de Don Bernardo de Cabrera* (1634). She goes over the situations, comparing the texts, judging finally, however, that Rotrou, by centering attention on a single problem, by observing the unities of time and place, and by stressing the psychological struggle instead of exciting incidents, produced a play of "more finished form" than the Spanish original.

[243] Jobit, Pierre. "Saint François de Sales et les influences espagnoles," *LLR*, III (1949), 83–104.

After sketching "le climat de spiritualité" of the period 1590 to 1600, the author examines the life of Saint François de Sales and considers the numerous Spanish influences which are revealed in the *Introduction à la vie dévote* and *Traité de l'amour de Dieu*, influences which de Sales himself acknowledged.

[244] Kaplan, D. "The Lover's Test Theme in Cervantes and Madame La Fayette," *FR*, XXVI (1952–1953), 285–290.

The result of Kaplan's investigation of the works of Cervantes and Mme de La Fayette which deal with this theme is a "plausible conclusion" that *El curioso impertinente* was influential on *Zayde* and thus on *La Princesse de Clèves*. Kaplan notes that scholarship has neglected this theme, which he believes is used by both Cervantes and Mme de La Fayette to point out the disastrous results of the compulsion to test love. He considers the Princesse de Clèves to be a counterpart of Anselmo in Cervantes' story.

[245] Kastner, L. E. "Concerning the Sonnet of the Sonnet," *MLR*, XI (1916), 205–211.

Kastner traces the various imitations of a sonnet by Lope de Vega, "Un soneto me manda hazer Violante," which in turn was an imitation of Diego Hurtado de Mendoza's "Pedís, reyna, un soneto; ya le hago." Kastner finds the earliest French imitation to be by Regnier Desmarais. Other poets who found this theme fascinating were Voiture in France and John Payne Collier, Thomas Edwards, and James Gibson in England. Kastner furnishes several versions of the sonnets written on this theme, enunciated in Lope's first line.

[246] Knowles, Edwin B. "Allusions to *Don Quixote* before 1660," *PQ*, XX (1941), 573–586.

Up to this time, Knowles states, scholars had found thirty

allusions to the *Quijote* in English literature before the Restoration, mostly in drama. In this article he presents forty-nine "new" allusions, chiefly from nondramatic writings. These he lists with comments in chronological order and concludes that the pre-1660 allusions in general reveal a growing knowledge of Cervantes and dispel the old idea that *Don Quijote* became an instantaneous success in England. He points out that its best qualities—its satire, humor, and realism—were not really appreciated until after the Restoration.

[247] ———."*Don Quixote* through English Eyes," *Hispania*, XXIII (1940), 103–115.

The design of this article, in the author's words, is to present "a rapid summary of three major changes in English literary taste as it focussed itself on this one Spanish work." He presents the three interpretations of Cervantes' novel as being: (1) in pre-Restoration days, a jestbook; (2) in the eighteenth century, a humorous satire popular with all classes; (3) in the Romantic era, a sad comment on human idealism. Twentieth-century taste, Knowles remarks, encompasses all interpretations.

[248] Lancaster, H. Carrington. "Boisrobert's *Vraye Didon*: A Reply," *RR*, XXXIII (1942), 72–73.

This article forms a reply to Eyer's article in *RR*, 1941 (q.v.). Lancaster declares that Eyer has to depend solely on internal evidence to prove that Boisrobert was influenced by sixteenth-century Spanish dramatists. It is Lancaster's opinion that Eyer's verse quotations are not similar enough to prove more "than that the two dramatists Lasso de la Vega and Boisrobert had in common ideas that would readily be suggested by a reading of Justin and Vergil" and "no more can be said in regard to Virués' play, which resembles Boisrobert's still less."

[249] ———. "Calderón, Boursault, and Ravenscroft," *MLN*, LI (1936), 523–538.

Lancaster calls Boursault's *Ne pas croire ce qu'on voit, histoire espagnole* (1670), a satírico-romantic novel and a

"curious example of French-Spanish, Spanish-French relations." He concludes that when Boursault refers to a Spanish original that he used for a source, he means Calderón's
Casa con dos puertas. Too, Lancaster sees direct relationships among these two works and Ravenscroft's *Wrangling
Lovers.*

[250] ———. "Castillo Solórzano's *El Celoso hasta la muerte* and
Montfleury's *École des jaloux,*" MLN, LIV (1939), 436–437.
Lancaster rejects the theory held by Adolphe de Puibusque that Lope de Vega's *Argel fingido* was the source of
Montfleury's play. He shows that the French writer takes his
plot from Solórzano's *novela* about a jealous husband, as
well as taking the name and character of the hero and details
of dialogue.

[251] ———. "Don Juan in a French Play of 1630," PMLA, XXXVIII
(1923), 471–478.
An attempt to establish the influence of *El Burlador de
Sevilla* of Tirso de Molina on a French play by La Croix,
L'inconstance punie. Lancaster believes that the influence of
El Burlador was felt earlier than heretofore thought likely,
although he admits that proof of his theory that an Italian
play served as an intermediary has not been established.

[252] ———. "Lope's *Peregrino,* Hardy, Rotrou, and Beys," MLN, L
(1935), 75–77.
Lancaster announces his discovery that the chief source of
Hardy's tragedy *Lucrèce* (1628), that of Beys' tragi-comedy
Hôpital des fous (1635), and a partial source of Rotrou's
Céliane are to be found in Lope de Vega's *El Peregrino en su
patria* (1604). This article sets forth details in order to compare these works and notes that *El Peregrino* seems to have
been the first of Lope's writings to influence a French dramatist. Lancaster states that "now we know the sources of
all of Hardy's extant tragedies."

[253] ———. "Reply to Footnote on Calderón, Ravenscroft, and
Boursault," MLN, LXIII (1948), 219–220.
Lancaster once more replies in the debate with J. U.

Rundle (see entries 322, 323) concerning the Spanish, English, and French writers in the title. Although nothing has been decided, the discussion does shed light on the methods of subtle scholarly invective.

[254] ———. "Still More about Calderón, Boursault, and Ravenscroft," *MLN*, LXII (1947), 385–389.

A reply to James Urvin Rundle's article in *MLN*, 1947 (q.v.), in which Rundle declares that Ravenscroft did not imitate Boursault as Lancaster had stated in a previous article in *MLN*, 1963 (q.v.). Lancaster advises Rundle to seek the unknown Spanish novel which Rundle suggested might be the source of *The Wrangling Lovers* by Ravenscroft.

[255] ———. "The Origin of the Lyric Monologue in the French Classical Tragedy," *PMLA*, XLII (1927), 782–787.

Lancaster discounts the idea that the French lyric monologue evolved from the Spanish sonnet-monologue, taking objection to scholars' inclination to exclaim "Cherchez l'espagnole," whenever they are in doubt as to a phenomenon in a French classical play. He cites Martinenche's interpretation of Corneille's use of *stances* as a case in point. In defense of his own position Lancaster avers that of 117 extant French plays written between 1628 and 1634 in which the lyric monologue was used, at the most eight plays show Spanish influence.

[256] ———. "The Ultimate Source of Rotrou's *Venceslas* and of Rojas Zorrilla's *No hay ser padre siendo rey*," *MP*, XV (1947), 435–440.

Lancaster here identifies the historical event from which Rojas Zorrilla derived the plot of his play, discovering that it is based on an incident in Bohemian history. He emphasizes, too, the imitative nature of Rotrou's *Venceslas*, for he sees it as being based on *No hay ser padre siendo rey*.

[257] Lanson, Gustave. "Études sur les rapports de la littérature française et de la littérature espagnole au XVIIe siècle," *RHLF*, III (1896), 45–70.

This excellent article is the first of a series. Lanson acknowledges the work of Morillot, Claretie, Roy, and Reynier, who have presented scholarly studies on Scarron, Lesage, Sorel, and Thomas Corneille, and gives a comprehensive survey of the Spanish influence in the period 1600–1660. This study is divided in two parts: Part I—"Antonio Pérez et les origines de la préciosité"; Part II—"Diffusion de la langue et de la littérature espagnole." In regard to Pérez, Lanson states that he is not, as was commonly held, the initiator of *la préciosité*.

[258] ———. "Études sur les rapports de la littérature française et de la littérature espagnole au XVIIᵉ siècle," *RHLF*, III (1896), 321–331.

This part of Lanson's series is concerned with "Poètes espagnoles et poètes françaises." Góngora and Scarron are compared, and Lanson states, "La véritable imitateur de Góngora chez nous, c'est Scarron," giving careful attention to the characteristics of Góngora's poetry which influenced the French writer.

[259] ———. "Études sur les rapports de la littérature française et de la littérature espagnole au XVIIᵉ siècle," *RHLF*, IV (1897), 61–73.

This article continues the study of French poets in relation to their Spanish influences. Lanson studies Bertaut and Desportes and finds indications of inspiration from Montemayor in Desportes, but in Bertaut no certain ones. He notes that Malherbe, too, in his *Commentaire*, sees the influence of the *Diana* of Montemayor on Desportes.

[260] ———. "Études sur les rapports de la littérature française et de la littérature espagnole au XVIIᵉ siècle," *RHLF*, IV (1897), 180–194.

The French writer Voiture is studied in this section of Lanson's series. He sees Voiture as being influenced more by the Spanish than by the Italians and mentions among others the Spaniards Pérez de Hita, Góngora, Castillejo, and Lope de Vega as writers admired by the French author.

[261] ————. "Études sur les rapports de la littérature française et de la littérature espagnole au XVIIᵉ siècle," *RHLF*, VIII (1901), 395–407.

A study of Sarasin concludes this scholarly series of articles on Spanish-French literary relations. Lanson says that although Sarasin modeled most of his works on classical lines, he did not conceal his admiration for the Spanish, whose works he could read in the original. Lanson remarks, "Les Espagnols l'avaient aidé à affiner son esprit, à polir son style."

[262] Lapp, J. C. "The Defeat of the Spanish Armada in French Poetry of the XVIth Century," *JEGP*, XLIII (1944), 98–100.

Lapp comments on the "curious" fact that "one of the greatest events in English history received its worthiest treatment in the obscure pages of Pierre Poupu's *Muse Chrestienne*, published in 1590." Poupu was a Huguenot who was naturally overjoyed at the defeat of the erstwhile proud Spanish navy. This article provides an interesting sidelight on an event so important to Spain, England, and France, and brings attention to a little-known work of literature.

[263] Lida de Malkiel, Maria Rosa. "De Centurio al Mariscal de Turena: Fortuna de una frase de *La Celestina*," *HR*, XXVII (1959), 150–166.

The author presents an intensive study of the words spoken by Centurio (*Celestina*, XVIII, 180), "Yo te juro por el sancto martilogio de pe a pa, el braço me tiembla de lo que por ella entiendo hazer," showing how this idea is reflected in subsequent dramatic works, including some of the French writers Brantôme, Desportes, Taillebras, and Corneille. Short quotations are used in illustration.

[264] ————. "Para las fuentes españolas de algunos sonetos burlescos de Scarron," *RLC*, XXVII (1953), 185–191.

The author contrasts some poetry of Lope de Vega with some of Scarron's and concludes that the tone of the former is much more elevated, presenting in illustration a sonnet of Lope and one of Scarron and pointing out that Scarron, although influenced by Spanish models, injected his own kind of "sátira francesa" into his finished sonnet.

[265] Linsalata, Carmine R. "Smollett's Indebtedness to Jarvis' Translation of *Don Quijote*," *Symposium*, IV (May 1950), 84–106.

In 1749 Tobias Smollett, as Linsalata points out, was commissioned by a group of booksellers to translate *Don Quijote*, but the work did not appear until 1755. Linsalata presents here a painstaking study to review the historical background of this 1755 translation, showing that Smollett drew freely from Jarvis' translation of 1742, since it is probable that Smollett did not know Spanish well enough to translate Cervantes adequately. The author provides excerpts from Cervantes' text, Jarvis' rendition, and Smollett's version, expressing his opinion that Jarvis' work is superior to Smollett's. This study is well documented.

[266] Lister, J. T. "A Comparison of Two Works of Cervantes with a Play by Massinger," *Hispania*, V (May 1922), 133–140.

A comparison of the *novela El Celoso Estremeño* and the farce *El Viejo celoso* of Cervantes with each other, and a contrast of these two with *The Fatal Dowry* by Philip Massinger, in order to determine if there are any connections between these works of the two writers. After a detailed consideration of the plots and characterization in the plays, Lister concludes that what slight connection there is can be traced to the inclusion of the Spanish point-of-honor theme, but he believes that the difference of treatment given to this by Cervantes and the treatment given by Massinger makes it seem unlikely that the English writer was imitating Cervantes directly, even though it is possible that Massinger knew the two Cervantine pieces considered here.

[267] Loftis, John. "Spanish Drama in Neo-Classical England," *CL*, XI (1959), 29–34.

Remarking that many English Restoration and eighteenth-century dramas are based on Spanish plays and adapted to conform to French rules, Loftis uses as prime examples *The Counterfeits* (1678) of John Leanerd and Colley Cibber's *She*

Would and She Would Not, which he sees as imitative of Moreto's *La ocasión hace al ladrón* and Tirso's *Don Gil de las calzas verdes*, respectively.

[268]   McCann, Eleanor. "Donne and Saint Teresa on the Ecstasy," *HLQ*, XVII (1954), 125–132.

Miss McCann contends that even if Donne's indebtedness to Saint Teresa cannot be clearly proved, the close similarities between the two claim attention as at least a startling literary coincidence. They seem to be "fighting the same battle, one a Renaissance saint, one a sinner." Objects of this study are the *Ecstasy* of Donne and the middle portion of Saint Teresa's *Vida*.

[269]   ————. "Oxymora in Spanish Mystics and English Metaphysical Writers," *CL*, XIII (1961), 16–25.

Miss McCann's concern is with tracing the possible influences of such Spanish mystics as Santa Teresa de Avila, Diego de Estella, Luis de León, and Juan de la Cruz upon some English writers, notably Robert Southwell, John Donne, Richard Crashaw, Joseph Beaumont, and Henry Vaughn. This article studies the use of oxymora by the writers, characterizing the device as "half-rhetoric, half-philosophy," and points out that such expressions as "dying life," "sweet wounds," "blind vision," are a natural way of expressing a core idea of Spanish mysticism—namely, that the unifying force of God blots out apparent contrarieties in the mind of the devout. Miss McCann points out that Southwell introduced the "tears theme of penitent literature" into English poetry with his translation of Diego de Estella's *Meditaciones devotísimas del amor de Dios*, that Joseph Beaumont was a pioneer scholar of Spanish mysticism, and that John Donne traveled in Spain. Quotations from the English poets are used to illustrate Miss McCann's statements.

[270]   M'Carthy, D. F. Letter to the Editor, *Athenaeum*, XXVI, Pt. 1 (1864), 440.

The correspondent argues against the fallacy that Cervantes and Shakespeare died on the same day, basing his reasoning on differences in the calendar reckonings of Spain and England at the time that these writers lived. M'Carthy declares that Shakespeare survived Cervantes by twelve days, since England did not adopt the Gregorian calendar until 1754.

[271] McClelland, I. L. "Tirso de Molina and the Eighteenth Century," *BHS*, XVIII (1941), 182–204.

Miss McClelland has divided her study of Tirso into two parts: (1) The Dramatic Ideal of the Eighteenth Century and (2) Tirso's Legacy to the Eighteenth Century. The first part presents Tirso's drama as incorporating the eighteenth-century heroic ideal, a model which was not recognized by the literary world of this time because of the admiration for Calderón. Miss McClelland's discussion of the eighteenth-century literary philosophy takes into consideration the Spanish, English, and French manifestations. In the second part of her article the author emphasizes again Calderón's preponderance and considers the reason for the neglect of Tirso, expressing her doubt that the *comedia* was ever a subtle enough vehicle for the complex Tirsian genius. She compares Tirso's subtlety to that of Shakespeare and relates the Tirsian economy of means to the ideals of the neo-classicists.

[272] McDiarmid, Matthew P. "The Spanish Plunder of William of Hawthornden," *MLR*, XLIV (1949), 17–25.

Calling William Drummond "one of the most thorough and successful exponents of the Renaissance practice of literary plunder," the author cites L. E. Kastner as showing that only about a score of Drummond's creations do not incorporate traces from Italian, French, Spanish, and English poets. As he examines the "Spanish plunder," McDiarmid notes that Drummond borrowed from such writers as Garcilaso de la Vega, Juan Boscán, Cristóbal de Castillejo, Gutierre de Cetina, and Hurtado de Mendoza. Drummond had a library which was probably better stocked with Spanish books than that of any equally famous contemporary; McDiarmid mentions many of them, in both poetry and prose.

[273]   McGhee, Dorothy M. "Voltaire's *Candide* and Gracián's *El Cri-ticón*," *PMLA*, LII (1937), 778–784.

Miss McGhee presents Gracián's work as one of the "probable" readings that went to make up Voltaire's *contes philosophiques*, especially *Candide*. Observing that these two writers should have been kindred spirits because of the "satiric pungency" which was found in the atmospheres of both seventeenth-century Spain and eighteenth-century France, the author presents many specific points of solid comparison between *El Criticón* and *Candide*.

[274]   MacMillan, Douglas. "The Sources of Dryden's *The Indian Emperour*," *HLQ*, XIII (1950), 355–370.

Disagreeing with previous appraisals of Dryden's sources for this play, the author proposes that the play was suggested by a play of Davenant and that its principal sources were the Spanish accounts found in *Purchas His Pilgrims* (1625), Purchas being a translator who combined the chronicles of Peru with those of Mexico. MacMillan thinks that Dryden might have taken the "bed of roses" speech directly from López de Gómara, if he did not take it from Purchas' translation.

[275]   Madariaga, Salvador de. "Don Quijote, europeo," *RO*, XVI, No. 48 (1967), 258–276.

An interestingly written article which sees Don Quijote from two perspectives: in the light of some literary ideas that existed in pre-Quijote days, and in the light of the influence of the ideas of "mad" Don Quijote upon future generations, ideas which are generally attributed to more recent figures, including, for example, Jean Jacques Rousseau. Madariaga sees Don Quijote as a "true European."

[276]   ———. "Inglaterra, Francia, España, su evolución histórica," *REH*, I (1928), 34–43.

Brief but valuable comments concerning one of the great turning points of the history of these nations, the era of the discovery of America. The author considers the attitudes prevailing in these countries and notes the role each played in the events of the time. Since the attitudes were reflected in contemporary literature, Madariaga's study should offer useful knowledge for the interpretation of themes then current.

[277]   Magnin, Charles. "Des Origines du théâtre en Europe," *RDM*, IV (décembre 1834), 578–597.

This article is based on the author's assertion that the influence of the Catholic Church has been crucial in the development of the European drama—"cette influence est un loi social" of all Christian countries—and it is necessary to understand the early church in order to comprehend intelligently the great works of Lope de Vega, Calderón, Shakespeare, Molière, Corneille, Racine, and their contemporaries.

[278]   Malkiewicz, Marie. "Un Remaniement français de *La Vie est un songe*," *RLC*, XIX (1939), 429–444.

The debt of L'abbé de Boisrobert, author of *La Vie n'est qu'un songe*, to Calderón is weighed by Miss Malkiewicz. Admitting that Boisrobert shows talent only of the second order in his collection of stories *Nouvelles héroïques et amoureuses* (1657), she finds interest in observing how he changed Calderón's *La Vida es sueño* to suit his purposes, one of the changes being the greater attention given to Poland in the work of the French writer. Miss Malkiewicz notes, "Il est intéressant de rencontrer la Pologne dans les relations littéraires entre la France et l'Espagne."

[279]   Margouliès, G. "Scarron et Lope de Vega, " *RLC*, VIII (1928), 511–515.

Noting that Scarron imitated to a very great extent the works of Lope de Vega, Margouliès presents three sonnets by Scarron and the poems of Lope which allegedly served as models. The author believes, too, that Scarron's "Un amas confus de maisons" is adapted from the Spanish, but at this writing he is unable to identify the exact source.

[280]   ———. "Scarron sonnettiste et ses modèles espagnoles," *RLC*, XIII (1933), 137–138.

The author corrects his statement made in a previous article (see above) that Scarron's sonnet, "Un amas confus de maisons," was probably written in imitation of Lope de Vega by stating now that it is Luis de Góngora that Scarron has emulated by presenting as evidence the text of Scarron's sonnet and one of Góngora's, "Una vida bestial de encantamiento."

[281] Martin, H. M. "Corneille's *Andromède* and Calderón's *Las Fortunas de Perseo*," MP, XXIII (1925–1926), 407–415.

The author argues that Corneille may have influenced Calderón, contrary to the general supposition that Corneille was influenced by the Spanish writer. Martin presents evidence to support his argument that Calderón knew the French language and read contemporary French literature, believing too facile the assumption that Calderón did not.

[282] Martinenche, Ernest. "Les Sources de *l'École des maris*," RHLF, V (15 janvier 1898), 110–116.

Interesting comments upon Molière's use of the age-old theme of the delicate ruses of women. Martinenche sees Molière as "habile directeur de troupe," taking hints from the Spaniards, especially Hurtado de Mendoza and Lope de Vega, as well as from his French contemporaries, who were in turn influenced by Spanish dramatists, for example, Boisrobert, whose *La folle gageure* owes something to Lope's *El Mayor imposible*.

[283] ———. "Les Sources espagnoles de *Horace* et d'*Héraclius*," RLR, XLIII (1900), 262–268.

Martinenche purports to show that Corneille conceived these two plays in his imagination only after reading two Spanish *comedias*, *El honrado hermano* of Lope de Vega and Calderón's *En esta vida todo es verdad y todo mentira*, and adds that "l'originalité de Pierre Corneille n'a rien à perdre à cette rapide étude," since Corneille is one of those who "enrichissent quand ils dérobent."

[284] Matthews, W. "Samuel Pepys and Spain," *Neophilologus*, XX (1934), 120–129.

Matthews reflects upon how brilliant a picture of Spain we would have had if the qualities that made the *Diary* so famous had been found in Pepys' notes upon Spain. Nevertheless, the impressions he did record are of interest to students of literature and history alike, for they do reflect this Englishman's curiosity concerning certain aspects of Spanish culture. Pepys' visit, which had for purpose the carrying out of an official governmental errand, was made in 1683. Upon his return the diarist carried with him some chapbooks which were being widely circulated in Spain.

[285]   Matulka, Barbara. "The Main Source of Scudéry's *Le Prince déguisé*—the *Primaleón*," *RR*, XXV (1934), 1–14.

Miss Matulka is convinced that Mlle de Scudéry must have been acquainted with the Spanish novel of chivalry *Primaleón*, for it was widely read in France after its translation in 1550. The main theme of *Le Prince déguisé* corresponds exactly to the adventures of the hero in the Spanish novel, Miss Matulka notes, as she presents evidence for this and for her contention also that Mlle de Scudéry has amalgamated several other themes to enhance her plot, themes taken from *Le Cid*, Juan de Flores' works, as well as some imitative of French and Italian authors.

[286]   Mesnard, Pierre. "La Philosophie politique espagnole au XVIIᵉ siècle," *DS*, XXVI (avril 1955), 178–184.

The theme of this article is, in the words of the author, "Le XVIIᵉ siècle français n'est pas seulement en continuité avec le XVIᵉ, mais aussi avec le XVIIᵉ siècle espagnol." Mesnard provides interesting historical background material for literary studies concerning the Spanish influence on the culture of France.

[287]   Michaud, G. L. "Luis Vives and Rabelais' Pedagogy," *PMLA*, XXXVIII (1923), 419–424.

Michaud makes the point that since Juan Luis Vives wrote his treatises on education before Rabelais wrote *Gargantua*, the similarities of ideas on pedagogy suggest that Rabelais took much from Vives. Michaud's research on this stems from a reading of an English version of Vives' *De Disciplines*, translated by Dr. Foster Watson in 1531, and from this work he quotes passages in which the ideas expressed correspond in "practically every point in Gargantua's so-called practical education."

[288] ———. "The Spanish Sources of Certain Sixteenth Century French Writers," *MLN*, XLIII (1928), 157–163.

An informative discussion of the debt owed to Spanish sources by many sixteenth-century French essayists, especially Pierre Bouaystuaux, Montaigne, Seigneur de Cholières, and Jean Bouchet. Cited as sources for these and others are Pedro Mexía, López de Gómara, Antonio de Guevara, Bartolomé de Las Casas, López de Castañeda, Antonio de Torquemada, Oviedo, Juan Vives, Rojas, and Juan de Dios Huarte. Michaud provides quotations from certain French and Spanish writers to illustrate their similarities. This study is well documented.

[289] Montégut, Émile. "Caractère historique et moral du Don Quichotte," *RDM*, C (ler mars 1864), 170–195.

Declaring that Don Quijote is a personage important not only in the literary history of Spain but in that of all Europe as well, Montégut devotes his thoughtful article to the delineation of Don Quijote's universal as well as his purely Spanish qualities, seeing him as a representative of mankind in addition to being a personification of Spain of the sixteenth century. He sees Don Quijote not as mad but as the victim of a hallucination.

[290] Morel-Fatio, Alfred. "Le troisième centenaire de Cervantes," *RDM*, XXXIII (mai–juin 1916), 591–619.

In this eulogy the author traces the fortunes of *Don Quijote* in France, beginning with its first translation in 1614 by César Oudin, interpreter for Louis XIII, a work which initiated a greater rapprochement of the two nations of France and Spain. France's knowledge of *Don Quijote* was preceded by England's, for in 1612 Thomas Shelton's edition had appeared. Morel-Fatio states that it was the English who first taught Spain to revere Cervantes. This article includes other extended commentaries on the value and meaning of *Don Quijote*.

[291] Morley, S. Griswold. "Notes on Spanish Sources of Molière," *PMLA*, XIX (1904), 270–290.

This article is the result of the author's research into passages from Molière's plays taken from Spanish literature or connected with it, but he does not pass judgment on whether or not there are "genuine instances of borrowing" or merely coincidences of thought and expression. Some of the parallels considered are: *Don Quijote* and *Le bourgeois gentilhomme*; the *Novelas* of Lugo y Dávila and *Le Misanthrope*; *El Burlador de Sevilla* and *Le Misanthrope*; *El Marqués de Alfarache* by Lope de Vega and *Le Festin de Pierre*.

[292] Muñoz Rojas, José A. "Un Libro español en la biblioteca de Donne," *RFE*, XXV (1941), 108–111.

Rojas concerns himself with a reference John Donne once made to a Spanish book, *Josefina*, in one of his sermons. In his copy of the book, which was published in 1609 by Fray Gerónimo Gracián, the English poet made marginal comments in Italian. Donne's copy may now be found in the British Museum.

[293] Myers, Oliver T. "Encina and Skelton," *Hispania*, XLVII (1964), 467–474.

Commenting that the literary historian can often find amazing parallels in the lives of pairs of men in different countries, Myers offers Juan del Encina (1468–1529?) and John Skelton (1460?–1529) as proof of this. He begins his analysis of this phenomenon with a consideration of the historical situation of Spain and England during the years of these men's lives, shows how both men became legends in their respective countries during their lifetimes and goes on to delineate their separate but similar works. Quotations from these works illustrate Myers' interesting thesis.

[294] Nelson, Lowry Jr. "Góngora and Milton: Toward a Definition of the Baroque," *CL*, VI (1954), 53–63.

The author compares the similar uses made of verb tenses by the two poets and gives examples from Góngora's "Polifemo" and Milton's "Nativity Ode." Nelson calls this use "confusionism," or "a battle of tenses going on, a battle for supremacy between present and past." He finds the basis of this common characteristic of Góngora and Milton in the specific concept of the baroque which was widespread in European literary thought of the times in which these poets lived. This article is a useful addition to other criticism which seeks to analyze the intellectual atmosphere of the later Renaissance.

[295]   Nethercot, Arthur H. "The Reputation of Native versus Foreign 'Metaphysical Poets' in England," *MLR*, XXV (1930), 152–164.

In the section of this article that treats of Góngora, Nethercot points out that the Spanish poet was often translated and imitated in England during the late Renaissance, but by the time of the Restoration he was attacked for so-called excesses of syle. During the age of Pope his poetry fell into deeper disgrace, and Góngora was contemned even more than the English Metaphysicals, in deference to the judgment of such arbiters as Samuel Johnson. Nethercot notes that when the vogue for metaphysical poetry was revived later on, Góngora did not share in the attention. He mentions as one factor causing this neglect the language barrier, for Góngora's strained, "conceited" style renders translation difficult.

[296]   Nozick, Martin. "The Inés de Castro Theme in European Literature," *CL*, III (1951), 330–341.

The story of Inés de Castro originated in Portugal, but Spanish versions of it, beginning with Gabriel Laso de la Vega's ballads (1587), are superior to the Portuguese, according to Nozick, and he states also that the Spanish versions preceded French and English works on this theme.

[297]   Oliphant, E. H. C. "Three Beaumont and Fletcher Plays," *RES*, XII (1936), 197–202.

In response to the article of R. Warwick Bond, "On Six Plays in Beaumont and Fletcher" (see entry 173), which Bond considers the Spanish sources of *Love's Cure*, Oliphant asserts that he would agree in the main but that he finds

Spanish influence only in Act II, sc. 2, and Act II, sc. 4, of *Love's Cure* and attributes the rest of Bond's references to English sources. Oliphant also objects to Bond's attribution of *Lazarillo de Tormes* to Hurtado de Mendoza.

[298]   Oppenheimer, Max Jr. "Supplementary Data on the French and English Adaptations of Calderón's *El Astrólogo fingido*," *RLC*, XXII (1948), 547–560.

   In Part I of this article the author takes a look at the French adaptations of *El Astrólogo fingido* made by Mlle de Scudéry, notably *Ibrahim*, and at D'Ouville's *Jodelet Astrologue*, commenting upon the changes made in the source play of Calderón. Part II examines the English adaptations, the anonymous *Feigned Astrologer* (directly founded on Thomas Corneille's *Le Feint Astrologue*) and Dryden's *An Evening's Love, or The Mock Astrologer*. Oppenheimer quotes Dryden's preface in which the dramatist anticipates charges of plagiarism. The article concludes with a bibliography of the adaptations of Calderón's play, including the French, English, Italian, Dutch, German, and Spanish ones. This is a thorough study which will be valuable for factual background in the comparative study of the drama of this period.

[299]   Parker, A. A. "Fielding and the Structure of *Don Quijote*," *BHS*, XXXIII (1956), 1–16.

   Parker finds the source of dissimilarity between Cervantes and Fielding in their techniques, their different approaches to the problem of constructing a novel. The rambling nature of *Joseph Andrews* imitates *Don Quijote*, but in *Tom Jones* Fielding "applies to the novel the rules of epic construction." Parker thinks that this gave formal neatness but sacrificed inner significance and calls the structure of *Don Quijote* a superior art-form.

[300]   ———. "Henry VIII in Shakespeare and Calderón, an Appreciation of *La Cisma de Inglaterra*," *MLR*, XLIII (1948), 327–352.

   Parker says that Calderón's play has been dismissed as a "perversion of history" by Ticknor, but that he seeks the "deliberate reason" for which Calderón departs from fact.

He finds that it is possible that Calderón's motive was to present truer insights into history as a drama of human actions. Thus Parker would consider *La Cisma de Inglaterra* much more historical than *Henry VIII* of Shakespeare. Even if the reader finds this explanation unconvincing, he will derive benefit from the article, since it contains a detailed analysis of Calderón's play, presented in the light of what Parker wishes to demonstrate.

[301] ———. "Santos y bandoleros en el teatro español del siglo de oro," *Arbor*, XIII (1949), 395–416.

Parker points out that the theme of bandit turned saint is encountered only in Spanish literature. The works that contain this theme are just the ones that have amazed foreigners; therefore, the author ponders the question, Are the Spanish of a different type from the rest of European peoples? He sees this theme as an indication of the admiration of the Spaniard for the heroic concept of life and illustrates his point from Lope de Vega and Tirso de Molina, suggesting that Spanish bandits, being idealistic, are different from their counterparts in other countries.

[302] Parker, J. H. "A Possible Source of a 'jeu de scène' in Molière's *École des maris*," *MLN*, LV (1940), 453–454.

Commenting that resemblances have been found between the scene in *École des maris* where Isabella gives her hand to be kissed (II, 9) and a similar scene in Lope de Vega's *La discreta enamorada*, Parker sees a closer parallel between Molière's play and Juan Pérez de Montalbán's *No hay vida como la honra*, Act I. Montalbán's play appeared in 1632.

[303] Peers, E. Allison. "Aportación de los Hispanistas extranjeros al estudio de Cervantes," *RFE*, XXXII (1948), 151–188.

A survey of the work of foreign scholars devoted to Cervantine studies in France, England, Germany, and Italy. Peers begins with a general introduction, then divides his work into divisions by countries. The result is an essay rich in allusions to information for further research.

[304] ———. "Cervantes in England," *BHS*, XXIV (1947), 226–238.

Cervantes once in his life made a charming gesture to

England, states Peers, identifying this gesture as one imbedded in one of the *Novelas ejemplares*, *La Española inglesa*, in which Queen Elizabeth is idealized and an "English" character (named Ricaredo) is portrayed as courageous and magnanimous. Peers sees the political implications in this, noting that it was written after the Anglo-Spanish peace had been made; probably Cervantes meant it as a contribution to the cause of better international relations. The remainder of this article presents a useful survey of the English translators of Cervantes' works.

[305] Peery, William. "*The Curious Impertinent* in *Amends for Ladies*," HR, XIV (1946), 344–353.

Peery considers the opinion of scholars, held since 1691, that Nathaniel Field's play, which appeared in 1611, was based on *Don Quijote*. The author cautions against exaggerating this claim, and on the basis of internal evidence suggests that Field may have taken what seems to be Cervantine material from the anonymous *Second Maiden's Tragedy* (1611), since the extent of Field's acquaintance with Spanish is quite unknown; nor is it known whether or not he knew enough French to read a translation of Cervantes' novelette. In conclusion Peery would credit Cervantes' claim, however, saying that it is possible that Field could have heard the story, even if he had not read it.

[306] Peñuelas, Marcelino C. "Algo más sobre la picaresca: *Lázaro de Tormes* y *Jack Wilton* de Nashe (1594)," *Hispania*, XXXVII (1954), 443–445.

Peñuelas sees a basic difference between the Spanish picaresque novel of *Lazarillo de Tormes* and Nashe's *Jack Wilton*, the English version of the fortunes of a *pícaro*: "Lázaro se nos mete muy adentro y nos hace partícipes de sus desventuras. Hay en él calor humano. Jack nos deja fríos." The author supports his statement with several contrasts which may be of help to the student of this genre.

[307] Perott, Joseph de. "The Mirrour of Knighthood," RR, IV (1913), 397–402.

Perott calls the rendering of the romance of chivalry *Es-*

pejo de príncipes y caballeros into the English language "the most laborious undertaking of the Elizabethans in the way of direct translation from the Spanish," giving the dates of the various books (which are now in the Bodleian Library). He notes an allusion to the *Mirrour*, as it was called, in John Lyly's *Euphues* and sees echoes of it in Shakespeare's *Tempest* (I, ii, 275–296; III, ii, 144–152) and *Hamlet* (II, ii, 334). As specimens of the English translation Perott gives passages from the story of the *Unfaithful Lover* along with the original Spanish text.

[308]   Petrie, Charles. "Paralelismo en la evolución histórica de Inglaterra y España," *Clavileño*, V, No. 28 (1954), 8–13.

An enlightening survey which stresses the parallels in the development of the two nations. Noting the reign of Henry VI in England and that of Ferdinand and Isabella in Spain, Petrie shows them as turning points in the nations' rise, critical periods which stimulated the creation of great literature.

[309]   Place, Edwin B. "A Note on *El Diablo cojuelo* and the French Sketch of Manners and Types," *Hispania*, XIX (1936), 234–240.

Place supplements and amplifies certain phases of the work of W. S. Hendrix on Guevara (q.v.) dealing with the theme of the Crippled Devil as an observer and satirist of manners, a theme which came from Spain to France and later to England. Place discusses several French works treating this theme.

[310]   ———. "El *Amadís* de Montalvo como manual de cortesanía en Francia," *RFE*, XXXVIII (1954), 151–169.

A well-documented study of the great impetus given to urbane manners in France by the Montalvo book and its translations. Place compares Montalvo's work with the translation of Herberay des Essarts, citing similar passages from the *Amadís* and *Le Trésor d'Amadis* (1559). Valuable bibliographical notes are included.

[311]   ———. "Una nota sobre las fuentes españolas de *Les Nouvelles* de Nicolas Lancelot," *RFE*, XIII (1926), 65–66.

Place's scrutiny of Lancelot's work, which appeared in 1628, leads him to believe that of the six novels included in *Les Nouvelles* at least five were translated from the Spanish, and he identifies the sources as Lugo y Dávila's *Teatro popular*, which includes several short works, and *Del andrógino* by Angelo Feren-Zuola.

[312] Praz, M. "Stanley, Sherburne, and Ayres as Translators and Imitators of Italian, Spanish, and French Poets," *MLR*, XX (1925), 280–294; 419–431.

Praz' motives in writing this two-part study are: (1) to emphasize the importance of Thomas Stanley's position as a promoter of the study of foreign poets (he includes Spanish, French, and Italian); (2) to show which of Edward Sherburne's poems show foreign influences; and (3) to show Philip Ayres' indebtedness (in *Lyric Poems*, 1687) to Spanish and Italian sources. Praz presents passages from the English works and their foreign models in parallel columns and comments that Edward Sherburne is the most interesting from a comparative point of view.

[313] Pujals, Esteban. "Shakespeare y Lope de Vega," *ReL*, I (1952), 25–45.

A scholarly article which considers the various factors operative on the two dramatists and compares and contrasts them. Four divisions of the subject are presented: (1) "Perspectiva histórica," (2) "El marco de la época," (3) "Shakespeare y Lope de Vega," and (4) "Caracteres literarios." One of the contrasts which he finds basic to the understanding of these two writers is that "Shakespeare raramente se preocupa de la moral . . . no pretende ser otra cosa que un gran poeta de la naturaleza. Lope . . . comparte las mismas ideas que los hombres de su época, no tiene dudas que enturbien su pensamiento," noting also that Spain, in contrast to England, held to "un concepto del mundo firme y definido" during the seventeenth century.

[314] Randall, Dale B. J. "*Axa and the Prince*: A Rediscovered *Novela* and Its English Translator," *JEGP*, LX (1961), 48–55.

An examination of Gracián Dantisco's *Galateo Español*

(1595), which, translated into English by William Style in 1640, became *The Spanish Gallant*, designed to serve as a "courtesy book." The Spanish work was based on an Italian source, but the story of Axa, as told here, did not appear in the Italian version. Style included it as a kind of "romantic escape" story. Randall deals with the problems of the identity of the William Style who should get credit for this translation (although it has suffered neglect for a long time), since there are two men of the same name to be reckoned with in this connection.

[315]   Reichenberger, A. G. "The Uniqueness of the *Comedia*," *HR*, XXVII (1959), 303–316.

Stating his opinion that the *comedia*'s greatness is "precisely in its being an unsurpassed instrument of self-expression of a people," the author points up its essential qualities and contrasts it with the Greek and the Shakespearean drama. This study is useful to the understanding of the qualities that make the *comedia* "typically Spanish."

[316]   Reparaz-Ruiz, G. de, and H. E. Davis. "Hispanic and Hispanic-American Studies in France," *HAHR*, XXVI (1946), 425–436.

A useful enumeration of advances in Hispanic studies made by French scholars during the years 1939–45, when many scholarly pursuits were eclipsed by the events of the Second World War.

[317]   Rivaille, L. "*Le Cid* et les oeuvres antérieures de Corneille," *RHLF*, XLV (1938), 503–517.

In his analysis of *Le Cid* Rivaille points out that in some aspects of the work the influence of Guillén de Castro is shown, but that in its patterns, ideas, and modes of expression the play is typical of Corneille's earlier plays.

[318]   Rogers, Paul Patrick. "Spanish Influence on the Literature of France," *Hispania*, IX (1926), 205–236.

Rogers criticizes those who would deny the contribution of the Spanish to French literature and presents a thorough study to support his belief that France of the first half of the seventeenth century was a "France espagnole." The article includes an exhaustive list of French authors whose works exhibit Spanish influence, beginning with Herberay des Essarts' translation of *Amadís de Gaula*. Included also is a "working bibliography" of books whose subject is the effect of Spanish literature on the literature of France. H. Carrington Lancaster, in his article, "The Origin of the Lyric Monologue in French Classical Tragedy" (see entry 255), says that there are so many errors in this article that readers may be "seriously misled."

[319] Rosenbach, Abraham S. W. "The *Curious Impertinent* in English Dramatic Literature before Shelton's Translation of *Don Quixote*," *MLN*, XVII (1902), 358–367.

The focus of attention of the author, as he surveys the influence of the *Curious Impertinent* on Jacobin drama, is *The Second Maid's Tragedy*. Rosenbach finds this play indebted to Cervantes for plot and atmosphere. Even though it was published before Shelton's translation of *Don Quijote* appeared, Shelton had had his translation in manuscript form five or six years earlier; and, if the author of *The Second Maid's Tragedy* had not seen that and did not know Castilian, he could have read the *novela* in French, since an edition appeared in Paris in 1608. Rosenbach sees some of Cervantes' "felicitous metaphors" in the English play, as he sees Cervantine influence in Beaumont and Fletcher's *The Coxcomb* and Nathaniel Field's *Amends for Ladies*.

[320] Rubio, David. "The Soul of Spain," *Americas*, I (1945), 263–288.

Stating that an understanding of Spain is necessary in order to evaluate her contributions to the intellectual life of Europe in the seventeenth century, Rubio attempts to analyze the Spanish ethos, concluding that "the true philosophy of Spain is her mystical spirit," and goes on to explicate this in terms definitely favorable to the Spanish. The author would seem to be less than objective in his desire to praise the "soul" of Spain.

[321] Rundle, James Urvin. "D'Avenant's *The Man's the Master* and the Spanish Source," *MLN*, LXV (1950), 194–196.

In this article the author notes that although it is well

known that this play of Davenant is a fairly close adaptation of Scarron's *Jodelet, ou le maître valet*, which was in turn adapted from Rojas Zorrilla's *Donde hay agravios no hay celos*, scholarship has neglected to see the points of resemblance between the English and the Spanish plays. Rundle proceeds to fill this lack by quoting various parallel passages from *The Man's the Master* and Zorrilla's play, the like of which do not occur in *Jodelet*.

[322] ———. "Footnote on Calderón, Ravenscroft, and Boursault," *MLN*, LXIII (1948), 217–219.

Rundle continues the heated dialogue which began with H. Carrington Lancaster's article in *MLN*, 1936 (see entry 249), concerning the source of Ravenscroft's *The Wrangling Lovers*.

[323] ———. "More about Calderón, Boursault, and Ravenscroft," *MLN*, LXII (1947), 382–384.

The author objects to H. Carrington Lancaster's hypothesis (*MLN*, 1936 [q.v.]) concerning the relationships among Calderón's *Casa con dos puertas*, Boursault's *Ne pas croire ce qu'on voit*, and Ravenscroft's *The Wrangling Lovers*. Rundle sees Ravenscroft's work as directly imitative of an unknown Spanish novel, which Calderón also must have used for his above-mentioned play and for *Fuego de Dios en el querer bien*.

[324] ———. "The Source of Dryden's 'Comic Plot' in *The Assignation*," *MP*, XLV (1947–1948), 104–111.

Disagreeing with certain other critics, Rundle sees Dryden not as using Scarron's *Roman comique* as a source for the "comic plot," and states that he finds the origin in Calderón's *Con quien vengo vengo*, which Scarron himself had used. The article enumerates resemblances and contrasts in Scarron's and Calderón's plays, the elements Dryden took from Calderón, and the changes made by Dryden. Quotations from Calderón and Dryden are presented to show that Dryden took his material for *The Assignation* without using the French model.

[325] ————. "Wycherley and Calderón: A Source for *Love in a Wood*," *PMLA*, LXIV, Pt. 2 (1949), 701–707.

Rundle believes that the source for William Wycherley's first play, *Love in a Wood*, can be found in Calderón's *Mañanas de abril y mayo*. It is Rundle's opinion that Wycherley shows little real ability in his role as adapter, and he identifies *Love in a Wood* as the Restoration play which assimilates Spanish most poorly. Parallel quotations from *Love in a Wood* and *Mañanas de abril y mayo* illustrate Rundle's criticism. See below for P. F. Vernon's article refuting Rundle's opinion.

[326] Russell, P. E. "A Stuart Hispanist: James Mabbe," *BHS*, XXX (1953), 75–84.

It is Russell's opinion that there were many competent translators of Spanish books during the seventeenth century, but what distinguishes Mabbe is his "scholarly approach to the authors . . . , his understanding of what they were about and his insistence on translating not what was likely to be most popular but what he thought most worth translating." Russell believes that Mabbe deserves more recognition than he seems to have secured. This is a worthwhile article for the student of the history of translation.

[327] Salvio, Alfonso de. "Voltaire and Spain," *Hispania*, VII (1924), 69–110; 157–164.

A study in two parts of Voltaire's attitudes toward Spain and a discussion of the historical backgrounds of these attitudes, with a look at some of the most important sources used by Voltaire. Salvio points out that factors in Voltaire's prejudice against Spain included the fact that for 300 years France and Spain had been political enemies, with the Church and the Inquisition ever-present forces. The first part of the article is concerned mainly with social aspects of Voltaire's work on Spain, the second with his assessment of Spain's literary achievement. Careful documentation accompanies Salvio's statements.

[328] Sánchez y Escribano, F. "Actitud neoclásica de Voltaire ante el barroco español," *MLJ*, XXXVII (1953), 76–77.

The author points out the consistent negativism of Voltaire's literary philosophy as it concerned Spain. Especially virulent were the French writer's attacks on seventeenth-century Spanish drama. Sánchez compares him to Samuel Johnson, whose disdain for poets who ignored the "rules" is proverbial. A short but trenchant study.

[329] Sarrailh, Jean. "Lesage, adapteur d'Avellaneda," *BH*, LXVI (1964), 359–362.

Sarrailh notes that his attention was struck by "le singulier dénouement imaginé de toutes pièces par Lesage et totalement différent de celui d'Avellaneda," even though Lesage was supposedly translating the Spanish writer. Sarrailh concludes that Lesage's fertile imagination would not be circumscribed and, forgetting his author, the Frenchman adapted instead of translating.

[330] Schier, Donald. "Voltaire's Criticism of Calderón," *CL*, XI (1959), 340–346.

Since Voltaire applied strict neo-classical rules to Spanish literature, remarks Schier, he could come to nothing but unfavorable conclusions: *Don Quijote* was the only work that he would deign to praise. Schier sees Voltaire's general criticism severe but interesting and finds the critiques of Calderón's *La Devoción de la misa* and *En esta vida todo es verdad y todo mentira* are "unanswerable," since these plays are not among Calderón's masterpieces and would lend themselves easily to any firm criticism.

[331] Schoeck, R. J. "The Influence of *La Celestina* in England," *BPLQ*, VII (1955), 224–225.

Schoeck objects to Louis Ugalde's statement (see entry 347) that a pupil of Juan Luis Vives probably wrote the English interlude *Calisto and Melibea* (c. 1525), since Vives was at that time in Oxford. Schoeck sees no good reason for assuming this and also objects to Ugalde's remark that this interlude was the first English play to be based on a foreign source, for he sees an earlier French influence on Heywood's interludes. (See entry 346 for Ugalde's reply.)

[332] Segal, Erich. "Hero and Leander: Góngora and Marlowe," *CL*,
       XV (1963), 338–356.
       Observing that both Góngora and Marlowe approach the
       old Hero and Leander myth in a similar fashion by making
       it a mock epic, Segal states that this approach is "diametri-
       cally opposed to all previous treatments of the legend," and
       he contrasts the Spanish and the English writers by pointing
       out that "Góngora makes his characters mere types in a
       bourgeois travesty, while Marlowe exaggerates the sensual-
       ity of the lovers so that his entire poem resembles the fres-
       coes in the temple of Venus." Segal gives abundant
       quotations from *Hero y Leandro* and *Hero and Leander* to
       support the validity of his comparison of these two poets.

[333] Sender, Ramón. "Three Centuries of Don Juan," *BA*, XXIII
       (1949), 227–232.
       Sender presents a brief sketch of Don Juan's international
       fortunes which mentions various interpretations of the Don
       Juan theme as well as the numerous plays inspired by
       Tirso de Molina's *El Burlador de Sevilla* (1625?). Sender
       remarks that whereas the world never separates Don Quijote
       from Cervantes, "outside Spain no one remembers Tirso de
       Molina when Don Juan is mentioned."

[334] Shergold, N. D., and Peter Ure. "Dryden and Calderón: A New
       Spanish Source for *The Indian Emperour*," *MLR*, LXI (1966),
       369–383.
       The authors suggest that Dryden used Calderón's *El Prín-
       cipe constante* (ca. 1628) as a source for *The Indian Em-
       perour* (1665), which was a sequel to *The Indian Queen*.
       Shergold and Ure find the similarities chiefly in the plot
       structure, basing their reasoning on certain facts such as
       that three editions of Calderón's play had appeared in print
       by 1665 and that Dryden read Spanish and was much in-
       terested in Spanish literature, many times using Spanish
       settings for his plays and mentioning Spanish authors in
       his prefaces. Included in this article are key quotations from
       El Príncipe constante and *The Indian Emperour*; the foot-
       notes provide many items for further research.

[335] Simpson, Evelyn M. "Donne's Spanish Authors," *MLR*, XLIII (1948), 182–185.

Miss Simpson's point of departure for this article is the biography of Donne by Edmund Gosse, in which Gosse declares that Spanish literature was the main influence in Donne's development as a writer. Here the "structure of conjecture" which was built up is "over-confident," since she can find no valid evidence to support it. She calls for more research by a "well-qualified Spanish scholar" in the area of Góngora-Donne parallels.

[336] Singer, A. E. "The Literary Progeny of Cervantes: *El Licenciado vidriera*," *WVUB*, V (1947), 59–72.

Singer studies this *novela* of Cervantes from its earliest adaptation in 1653 by Moreto through its later versions and imitations by such French writers as Quinault and Molière. He cites as borrowed from Cervantes the sonnet scene in Molière's *Le Misanthrope*. Some attention is paid to the use English writers made of this popular *novela* which produced a variety of "literary progeny."

[337] Sloan, A. S. "Juan de Luna's *Lazarillo* and the French Translation of 1660," *MLN*, XXXVI (1921), 141–143.

Sloan comments upon an item in F. W. Chandler's bibliography in his *Romances of Roguery*, where Chandler states that the French translator who was responsible for the 1660 edition of *Lazarillo* used Juan de Luna's version from which to work. This article uses comparative quotations to illustrate Sloan's contention that another Spanish version must have been used.

[338] Smith, William F. "Vives and Montaigne as Educators," *Hispania*, XXIX (1946), 483–493.

Disagreeing with the commonly held idea that Montaigne was the first thinker to develop universal truths into a pedagogical system, Smith presents Juan Luis Vives as a claimant to this distinction and contrasts the Frenchman's system, which was aristocratic in bias, to the Spaniard's, which was democratic and more consonant with modern principles. The author notes that Montaigne was thirteen years old at the time of Vives' death and was not unfamiliar with Vives' work, for he cites the Spaniard in his essay "De la force de l'imagination." Smith provides a documentation from primary and secondary sources.

[339] Steiner, Arpad. "Calderón's *Astrólogo fingido* in France," *MP*, XXIV (1926–1927), 27–30.

Thomas Corneille's *Feint Astrologue* has been considered a mere translation of the Calderón play by many critics, but Steiner finds in the French play more emphasis on characterization and humor, and the differences lead him to believe that Corneille's plot came not directly from the Spanish but from Scudéry. He does, however, see Voltaire influenced by Calderón through the *Feint Astrologue*.

[340] Stout, Gardner D. Jr. "Some Borrowings in Sterne from Rabelais and Cervantes," *ELN*, III (1965), 111–118.

Abundant quotations from the primary works, Rabelais's *Gargantua and Pantagruel* and Cervantes' *Don Quijote*, illustrate in Stout's opinion "the remarkable capacity Sterne had for assimilating to his own purpose the many sources on which he drew." Cervantes was one of the authors of whose works Lawrence said he had conned "as much as his [pray'r] book." This study is well documented.

[341] Thomas, Henry. "Bibliographical Notes," *RH*, XLV (1919), 1–11.

The first of these "bibliographical notes" deals with "A Forgotten Translation of Cervantes," which refers to Roger Lestrange's *The Spanish Decameron* (1686), which contains five of Cervantes' *novelas* from the *Novelas ejemplares*, lifted by Lestrange from Mabbe's 1640 translation, and five of Solórzano's *novelas* from *Garduña de Sevilla*, taken from John Davies' 1665 translation. Thomas makes further comments regarding literary piracy in Lestrange's time.

[342] ———. "The English Translation of Quevedo's *La Vida del Buscón*," *RH*, LXXXI (1933), 282–299.

Thomas remarks that *La Vida del Buscón* was not the first of Quevedo's works to be translated into English, for the

English version of the *Sueños*, translated by Richard Cra-shaw as *Visions*, appeared in 1640, while *La Vida del Buscón* had to wait until 1657. Nor did *El Buscón* attain the popular-ity enjoyed by the other work. Thomas gives a list of English editions of this picaresque novel, accompanied by valuable commentaries.

[343] ————. "Three Translations of Góngora and Other Spanish Poets during the Seventeenth Century," *RH*, XLVIII (1920), 180–256; supplementary note, 311–316.

A pioneer work in the scholarship relative to the renewed interest in Góngora, this study covers the translations of the Spanish poet made by Thomas Stanley (1625–1678), Sir Richard Fanshawe (1608–1666), and Philip Ayres (1638–1712). Much of the value of this article lies in the copious examples of the poetry of Góngora which are juxtaposed with their translated counterparts in English.

[344] Thomas, Lucien-Paul. "François Bertaut et les conceptions dramatiques de Calderón," *RLC*, IV (1924), 199–221.

An examination of the reciprocal relations of Calderón and his admirer François Bertaut, who became acquainted with the Spanish writer while visiting in Spain. Thomas believes that Bertaut had an influence on Calderón's theories because of the discussion the two writers had on the "three unities" of neo-classical theory, not in a positive sense of adoption by Calderón, but with the result that Calderón was more convinced than ever of his own ideas regarding the need of the dramatist to exercise freedom in his creation.

[345] Turner, Philip A. "Sobre Pedro Mexía en Inglaterra," *NRFH*, III (1949), 275–278.

Turner inquires into the possible ways in which the "seven ages of man" idea could have come into English thought, especially in relation to the use made of it by Shake-speare for Jacques' speech in *As You Like It*. The author recapitulates the scholarship already done on this problem and states his preference for the theory that Shakespeare received his inspiration for this passage from Pedro Mexía's *Silva de varia lección* through an English version by Thomas

Miller, published in 1613–1619 but circulating in MS. many years earlier. Turner thinks it possible also that Shakespeare knew Sir Geoffrey Fenton's compilation of Guevara's work known in England as the *Golden Epistles*, which appeared in 1575.

[346] Ugalde, Louis. "A Reply," *BPLQ*, VII (1955), 226–227.

Ugalde replies to an article of R. J. Schoeck (entry 331) taking issue with certain of Ugalde's statements concerning an English interlude *Calisto and Melibea*, which was based on *La Celestina*. Ugalde admits with courtesy that his claim that a pupil of Vives wrote the interlude was not provable, and that he should have said that the interlude was the first English play indebted to a Spanish, not to any foreign, source.

[347] ———. "The *Celestina* of 1502," *BPLQ*, VI (1954), 206–222.

Ugalde considers the impact of *La Celestina* upon English drama, in the form of an interlude called *Calisto and Melibea* after the lovers in Rojas' work. He gives *La Celestina* credit for many firsts: the first English play indebted to a foreign source, the first contact of English and Spanish literature, the first play to suppress the allegory of the moralities, the play that marked the beginning of romantic comedy in England. Ugalde points out that by 1530 seventeen editions of this popular work had appeared in Spanish, along with many translations.

[348] Umphrey, George W. "Spanish Ballads in English: Part I, Historical Survey," *MLQ*, VI (1945), 479–494.

Commenting that "the charm of the old popular ballads of Spain has been felt more widely and deeply than has that of any other kind of Spanish poetry" and that these ballads resemble those of England in their human interest and dramatic directness, Umphrey notes with surprise that there is no recorded translation of Spanish ballads before 1765, the date of Percy's *Reliques*, a compilation which includes two ballads from the Spanish. Part I of this study (see No. 349, Part II) presents a chronology of ballad translations which have Spanish material; this listing covers the years

1765–1939. Included are appraisals of the work of the best translators, such as the eighteenth-century compilers Thomas Percy, John Pinkerton, and Thomas Rodd.

[349]   ——. "Spanish Ballads in English: Part II, Verse Technique," *MLQ*, VII (1946), 21–33.

Umphrey considers the problems of translating Spanish ballads into English and concludes that the most satisfactory rendition uses the technique of assonance in preference to consonantal rhyme, for this latter tends to become monotonous and so to minimize the charm of the poetry.

[350]   Valbuena Briones, A. "El Simbolismo en el teatro de Calderón. —La Caída del caballo," *RF*, LXXIV (1962), 60–76.

A comprehensive treatment of symbolic meanings common to Renaissance dramatists. The author selects several plays of Calderón in which horses are used with dramatic effect and shows how this equine theme is also used by Shakespeare, Corneille, Racine, and Marlowe as well as by Dante and classical writers.

[351]   Van Roosbroeck, Gustave L. "The Source of De Sallebray's *Amante Ennemie*," *MLN*, XXXVI (1921), 92–95.

This play, more important for its influence than for its intrinsic value, says Van Roosbroeck, is a stage adaptation of the novel *La Hayne et l'amour d'Arnoul et de Clairemonde* by Du Périer. This novel is the earliest example of the influence of the Spanish Cid tradition in France, antedating Castro's work by about fourteen years. The author finds many similarities between De Sallebray's *Amante Ennemie*, the *Mocedades*, and Corneille's *Le Cid*, but these similarities, he believes, are not due to direct imitation of either the Spanish or the French but to the influence of Du Périer's novel.

[352]   Verdevoye, Paul. "La Novela picaresca en Francia," *Clavileño*, VI, No. 35 (1955), 30–37.

Tracing the origins of the picaresque novel back to a thirteenth-century *fabliau* of Picardy, the author finds the origin of the word *pícaro* in *picard* and that this word "apareció en España solamente en el siglo XVI, precisamente cuando Picardía desempeñó su destacada en la historia franco-española." In the sixteenth and seventeenth centuries French translations of Spanish picaresque novels became important, beginning with the huge success of *Lazarillo de Tormes*. Verdevoye shows how intimately entwined were the Spanish and French threads of picaresque literature in the seventeenth century.

[353] Vermeylen, Alphonse. "Mystiques d'Espagne et de France," *LLR*, V (1951), 138–144.

Vermeylen gives credit to the Spanish mystics for inspiring their French counterparts. He summarizes the meager scholarship on this subject, the comparative literary influences of French and Spanish mystics. Here Vermeylen pays critical attention to the article of Helmet Hatzfeld "El estilo nacional en los símiles de los místicos españoles y franceses" (q.v.), pointing out its superficial treatment of the theme. Though in the form of a book review, this essay is worth reading for its explication of the concepts of mysticism.

[354] Vernon, P. F. "Wycherley's First Comedy and Its Spanish Source," *CL*, XVIII (1966), 132–144.

Vernon reconsiders the relationship, first noted by Rundle (*PMLA*, 1949, [entry 325]) between Wycherley's *Love in a Wood* and Calderón's *Mañanas de abril y mayo*, and at the same time seeks to refute Rundle's charge that Wycherly handled his Spanish material in an unsatisfactory manner.

[355] Vic, Jean. "La Composition et les sources du *Diable boiteux* de Lesage," *RHLF*, XXVII (1920), 481–517.

In Vic's opinion, the play *Le Diable boiteux* (1707) has been neglected in favor of *Gil Blas*, and so he presents a detailed analysis of it as a prelude to his study. Under "Les sources espagnoles" he mentions *El Diablo cojuelo* of Luis Vélez de Guevara (1641), which in turn was inspired by Quevedo's *Sueños*. The 1727 edition of *Le Diable boiteux* shows the effect of Francisco Santos, who in 1663 published *Día y noche de Madrid*, the probable influence on Lesage. Vic observes that the Spain depicted by Lesage is "de pure fantaisie," and he criticizes unfavorably the way Lesage handles his Spanish borrowings.

[356] Villarejo, Oscar M. "Shakespeare's *Romeo and Juliet:* Its Spanish Source," *SS*, XX (1967), 95–105.

Villarejo presents his reasons for adhering to the theory first set down by Julius Leopold Klein in his *Geschichte des Dramas* (Leipzig, 1874) that Shakespeare must have had an intimate knowledge of Lope de Vega's *Castelvines y Monteses* when he composed *Romeo and Juliet*. Villarejo's evidence, however, should be examined critically by the student.

[357] Walsh, James J. "Cervantes, Shakespeare, and Some Historical Backgrounds," *CW*, CIII (1916), 38–47.

Walsh gives some historical background in connection with the fallacy that Shakespeare and Cervantes died on the same day. He goes on to defend the Catholic Church in Spain for its lack of encouragement of education during the Renaissance and cites the merits of Spanish Renaissance writers as superior to those of the English writers of the same period, with the notable exception of Shakespeare, who, he declares, "was probably a Catholic." His contention that *Don Quijote* is "perhaps the most optimistic book in the world" may be questioned by some readers. A definitely biased article, but not without interest because of its controversial approach.

[358] Walton, L. B. "Two Allegorical Journeys: A Comparison between Bunyan's *Pilgrim's Progress* and Gracián's *El Criticón*," *BHS*, XXXVI (1959), 28–36.

Walton has written his article "to provide an example of how lines of thought, frequently similar, may be due to mere coincidence." He contrasts the figures of Bunyan and Gracián, characterizing them as "poles apart" in their intellectual milieu, religion, and interests: Bunyan was a practically unlettered Puritan, while Gracián was in the humanist tradition and a Catholic. Walton also compares and contrasts their literary methods, finding Gracián's psychological insights more subtle as both authors use similar allegorical devices, such as the metaphor of the world as a fair.

[359]   Watson, Foster. "Vives on Education," *JEGP*, XIV (1915), 271–274.

Watson emphasizes the role of Vives in molding educational theory in England, characterizing the Spanish humanist as the predecessor, for example, of Bacon in the advocacy of observation and experiment. Watson stresses, too, the importance of Vives' friendship with Thomas More, who shared Vives' views on pedagogy.

[360]   Williams, Grace Sara. "The *Amadís* Question," *RH*, XXI (1909), 1–168.

A detailed examination of the scholarship to date on the thorny *Amadís* question. Miss Williams begins with the earliest reference to the hero Amadís in 1350 and follows this lead through Montalvo's edition. On the way she analyzes the content of Arthurian romances from France and England and makes comparisons with the Spanish legends, finding many parallels in incidents, names, etc., and including many passages which illustrate her discoveries. A useful appendix gives a bibliography of *Amadís* editions chronologically arranged.

[361]   Wilson, Edward M. "Did John Fletcher Read Spanish?" *PQ*, XXVII (1948), 187–190.

"The scraps of more or less corrupt Spanish are not enough to provide evidence" that Fletcher knew Spanish, states Wilson. It is his opinion that Fletcher no doubt often used translations, although he may have known enough Spanish for his own purposes. Even though we do not have conclusive evidence for Fletcher's expert knowledge, Wilson would conclude that it is "simpler to believe that he read Spanish with some fluency than to postulate undiscovered translations or to invent unwanted collaborators."

[362]   ———. "Mr. Maugham and Spanish Literature," *Scrutiny*, IV (1935–1936), 209–213.

Wilson's review of Maugham's *Don Fernando* turns into

a little essay on Spanish-English literary relations. Noting the neglect of Spanish literature by modern Englishmen, Wilson declares that Maugham will do little to dispel the "black legend" surrounding things Spanish in English minds. He tries to dispel some of it, however, by comparing sixteenth- and seventeenth-century Spain and England, by pointing out the strong and fine tradition of the Spanish ballad, and by describing the universal appeal of Góngora, Lope de Vega, and Calderón. The article concludes with an appeal for language students who will learn Spanish for its literary value, not for "commercial reasons."

[363] ———. *"Rule a Wife and Have a Wife* and *El sagaz Estacio,"* RES, XXIV (1948), 189–194.

An attempt to prove that the main plot of Fletcher's play is derived from Alonso Jerónimo de Salas Barbadillo's novel *El sagaz Estacio, marido examinado,* a novel which, like *La Celestina,* is written in dialogue throughout. Wilson summarizes the main plot of the Spanish work and compares the incidents to specific examples in Fletcher's play.

[364] ———. Wilson, Edward M. "Some Poems from Samuel Pepys' Spanish Chap-books," BHS, XXXII (1955), 187–193.

In this article Wilson demonstrates the kind of reading matter "which almost illiterate classes of Spaniards bought and recited in the second half of the seventeenth century" as found in certain chapbooks (*pliegos sueltos*) which Pepys purchased in Seville and Cadiz early in 1684. Two poems in the collection, however, are ascribed to important Golden Age poets, perhaps Lope de Vega and Góngora.

Sources

The items for this bibliography have been derived in part from an examination of the following resources, indices, bibliographical works, and journals:

1. The card catalogs of the libraries of:
   Indiana University, Bloomington, Indiana
   Stetson University, DeLand, Florida
   University of Florida, Gainesville, Florida
   University of Michigan, Ann Arbor, Michigan
   University of Oregon, Eugene, Oregon
   University of Washington, Seattle, Washington
   Vanderbilt University, Nashville, Tennessee

2. Indices and bibliographies:
   Baldensperger, Fernand, and Werner P. Friederich. *Bibliography of Comparative Literature.* Chapel Hill, N.C.: The Orange Print-shop, 1960.
   Bateson, F. W., editor. *The Cambridge Bibliography of English Literature.* 4 vols. Cambridge and New York: The Macmillan Company, 1941.
   Berry, Lloyd E. *A Bibliography of Studies in Metaphysical Poetry, 1939–1960.* Madison: University of Wisconsin Press, 1964.
   Besterman, Theodore. *A World Bibliography of Bibliographies.* 4th ed., 5 vols.; Geneva and Lausanne: Societas Bibliographica, 1954–1966.
   Biblio. Catalogue des ouvrages parus en langue française dans le monde entier. Paris: Service Bibliographique de la Librairie Hachette, 1933——.
   Bond, Donald F. *A Reference Guide to English Studies.* Chicago and London: The University of Chicago Press, 1962.

Brach, O. M. Jr. *English Literature, 1660–1800: A Current Bibli-ography*. PQ, Supplement to Vol. XLV (1966), 491–602.

Brody, Jules, *et al.*, editors. *Bibliography of French Seventeenth Century Studies*. Published for the French III Committee of the Modern Language Association. Bloomington, Ind., 1954.

Cabeen, David C., and Jules Brody, editors. *A Critical Bibliog-raphy of French Literature*. Syracuse, N.Y.: Syracuse University Press, 1961.

Chandler, Richard E., and Kessel Schwartz. *A New History of Spanish Literature*. Baton Rouge: Louisiana State University Press, 1961.

Cioranescu, Alexandre. *Bibliographie de la littérature française du seizième siècle*. Paris: Librairie C. Klincksieck, 1959.

Delk, Lois Jo, and James Neal Greer. *Spanish Language and Liter-ature in the Publications of American Universities: A Bibli-ography*. Austin, Texas: University of Texas Press, 1954.

Dissertation Abstracts: A Guide to Dissertations and Monographs Available in Microfilm. Ann Arbor, Mich.: University Micro-films, 1952——.

Farinelli, Arturo. *Divagaciones hispánicas: Discursos y estudios críticos*. Barcelona: Imprenta Claraso, 1936.

Foulché-Delbosc, Isabel, and Julio Puyol. *Bibliografía de R. Foulché-Delbosc*. Madrid: Tipografía de la Revista Archivos, Bibliotecas, y Museos, 1931.

Foulché-Delbosc, R., and L. Barrau-Dihigo. *Manuel de l'hispan-isant*. 2 vols. New York: The Hispanic Society of America, 1920, 1925.

Friederich, W. P., editor. *Yearbook of Comparative and General Literature*. (After 1961 edited by Horst Frenz.) Chapel Hill: Uni-versity of North Carolina Press, 1951–1960.

Gaudin, Lois Strong. *Bibliography of Franco-Spanish Literary Re-lations (until the XIXth Century)*. Publications of the Institute of French Studies, Inc., Columbia University, New York. Bordeaux: Imprimerie Cadoret, 1930.

Golden, Herbert H., and Seymour O. Simches. *Modern French Literature and Language: A Bibliography of Homage Studies*. Cambridge, Mass.: Harvard University Press, 1953.

——. *Modern Iberian Language and Literature: A Bibliography of Homage Studies*. Cambridge, Mass.: Harvard University Press, 1958.

Grismer, Raymond. *A Bibliography of Articles on Spanish Literature*. Minneapolis: Burgess Publishing Co., 1933, 1945.

Hopper, Vincent F., and Bernard D. N. Grebanier. *Bibliography of European Literature*. Great Neck, N.Y.: Barron's Educational Series, Inc., 1954.

McCready, Warren T. *Bibliografía temática de Estudios sobre el Teatro Español Antiguo*. Toronto, Canada: University of Toronto Press, 1966.

Modern Humanities Research Association. *Annual Bibliography of English Language and Literature*. Cambridge, England: 1920——.

Modern Language Association of America. *Annual Bibliography*. Published in the April issue of *PMLA*. New York: 1921——.

——. *MLA International Bibliography of Books and Articles in the Modern Languages*. New York: 1963——.

Palfrey, Thomas R., *et al. Bibliographical Guide to the Romance Languages and Literatures*. Evanston, Ill.: Chandler's, Inc., 1951.

Parker, J. J., and A. G. Reichenberger. "A Current Bibliography of Foreign Publications Dealing with the *Comedia.*" *Bulletin of the Comediantes*, IV (1942).

Saintonge, Paul, and Robert Wilson Christ. *Fifty Years of Molière Studies: A Bibliography, 1892–1941*. Baltimore, Md.: Johns Hopkins Press, 1942.

Sears, Minnie E., and Marian Shaw, compilers. *Essay and General Literature Index*. (After 1934 compiled by Marian Shaw.) New York: H. W. Wilson, 1900——.

Serís, Homero. *Manual de bibliografía de la literatura española*. Syracuse, N.Y.: Centro de Estudios Hispánicos, 1948.

Simón Díaz, José. *Bibliografía de la literatura hispánica*. Madrid: Consejo Superior de Investigaciones Científicas, Instituto "Miguel de Cervantes," de Filológia Hispánica, 1950–61.

——. *Manual de bibliografía hispánica*. Barcelona: Editorial Gustavo Gills, S.A., 1963.

Social Sciences and Humanities Index. New York: H. W. Wilson Co., 1907——.

Van Tieghem, Paul. *La Littérature comparée*. Paris: A. Colin, 1951.

Vitale, Philip H. *Basic Tools of Research*. Great Neck, N.Y.: Barron's Educational Series, Inc., 1963.

Winchell, Constance M. *Guide to Reference Books*. 7th ed.

Chicago: American Library Association, 1951; Supplements, 1954–62.

3. Periodicals:
Americas (New York)
Arbor (Madrid)
Athenaeum (London)
Books Abroad (Norman, Oklahoma)
Boston Public Library Quarterly (Boston)
Bulletin Hispanique (Bordeaux, France)
Bulletin of Hispanic Studies (also *Bulletin of Spanish Studies*) (Liverpool, England)
Bulletin of the Comediantes (Madison, Wisconsin)
Catholic World (New York)
Clavileño (Madrid)
Comparative Literature (Eugene, Oregon)
Dix-Septième Siècle (Paris)
English Association Pamphlet (London)
English Language Notes (Boulder, Colorado)
English Literary History (Baltimore, Maryland)
Europe (Paris)
Fortnightly Review (London)
French Review (Baltimore, Maryland)
Hispania (Appleton, Wisconsin)
Hispanic American Historical Review (Durham, North Carolina, and Baltimore, Maryland)
Hispanic Review (Philadelphia, Pennsylvania)
Huntington Library Quarterly (San Marino, California)
Insula (Madrid)
Journal des Savants (Paris)
Journal of English and Germanic Philology (Urbana, Illinois)
Les Lettres Romanes (Louvain, Belgium)
London Times Literary Supplement (London)
Modern Language Journal (Washington, D.C.)
Modern Language Notes (Baltimore, Maryland)
Modern Language Quarterly (Seattle, Washington)
Modern Language Review (Cambridge, England)
Modern Languages (London)
Modern Philology (Chicago, Illinois)
Neophilologus (Groningen, The Netherlands)

Notes and Queries (London)
Nueva Revista de Filología Hispánica, (Guanajuato, Mexico)
Philological Quarterly (Iowa City, Iowa)
PMLA—Publications of the Modern Language Association of America (New York)
Proceedings of the British Academy (London)
Review of English Studies (London)
Revista de España (Madrid)
Revista de Estudios Hispánicos (Puerto Rico)
Revista de Filología Española (Madrid)
Revista de Literatura (Madrid)
Revista de Occidente (Madrid)
Revue Bleue (Paris)
Revue d'Histoire Littéraire de la France (Paris)
Revue de Littérature Comparée (Paris)
Revue des Deux Mondes (Paris)
Revue des Langues Romanes (Montpellier, France)
Revue Hispanique (New York)
Romanic Review (New York)
Romanische Forschungen (Frankfurt am Main, Germany)
Romanistisches Jahrbuch (Hamburg, Germany)
Scrutiny (Cambridge, England)
Shakespeare Quarterly (New York)
Shakespeare Survey (Cambridge, England)
Studies in Philology (Chapel Hill, North Carolina)
University of Texas Bulletin (Austin, Texas)
West Virginia University Bulletin (Morgantown, West Virginia)

Index

136